THE ANSWER MODEL THEORY

John Montgomery and Todd Ritchey

TAM Books

John Montgomery and Todd Ritchey

Contents

Summary

We suggest that all dysfunctional behaviors, including those associated with various neuroses and psychopathologies, are driven and sustained by biochemical addiction. Addictive drugs trigger the release of dopamine and ß-endorphin in various reward areas of the brain, and are thought to create addictive states by hijacking the neural circuits that evolved to motivate and reward behaviors critical to survival and reproduction. A number of studies have shown that non-homeostatic states – states of physical or emotional distress – also trigger the release of dopamine and ß-endorphin in reward areas. We propose that persistent states of non-homeostasis can create a biochemical addiction to such states by similarly hijacking the brain's core survival responses. Such addictions, we suggest, are responsible for a wide variety of behavioral dysfunctions, including the "repetition compulsion," dysfunctional relationship "dramas," and eating disorders. These addictions also frequently subvert the adaptive functions of sleep, dreaming, play behavior, and the recently evolved human capacities for "mental time travel" and "theory of mind." We further suggest that nearly all addictions arise in response to the unnatural circumstances found in post-agricultural societies.

Introduction

One of the key drives in any living system is the drive to achieve and maintain balance, or homeostasis. In simple organisms, the homeostatic drive acts at a cellular level to automatically restore the proper balance of minerals and biomolecules within each cell. But in higher animals, more complicated functions – such as the capacity to experience subtle emotional states that may, in turn, result in specific decisions or physical actions – are also geared towards the maintenance of homeostasis.[1] Human beings experience homeostasis as a feeling of peace or well-being, or of emotional and physical balance. The homeostatic drive serves to maintain homeostasis both at these higher levels and also at the lower, cellular levels. Biochemical addiction, we suggest, represents a *non*-homeostatic drive – that is, biochemical addiction dysfunctionally drives an animal or human being away from biochemical and psychological balance. This dysfunctional drive may be expressed as an addiction to drugs of abuse, but also, we suggest, as an addiction to emotionally and physically non-homeostatic states. States of non-homeostasis, such as anxiety or anger, appear to always involve a stress response, and a number of studies have shown that stress hormones like cortisol have effects on the brain's reward system that are very similar to the effects of cocaine, methamphetamine and other addictive drugs.[2]

A variety of painful or distressing physical and emotional states have also been shown to trigger the release of the opioid ß-endorphin, which appears to be the primary neurochemical that mediates the feeling of pleasure or euphoria in all mammals, including humans.[3] We suggest that this seemingly paradoxical evolutionary quirk – that painful or distressing states also produce the key neurochemical that mediates the feeling of pleasure – ultimately explains all, or nearly all, dysfunctional behavior in human beings. Furthermore, we propose that painful or distressing states, and the biochemical rewards these states supply, can become behaviorally reinforced because, like addictive drugs, they hijack the survival instincts that are mediated by the reward system.

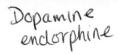

Addiction and the Reward System

A number of studies have indicated that the most important neurochemicals involved in drug addiction are the neurotransmitter dopamine and the endogenous opioid, ß-endorphin.[4] Drugs are thought to create addictive states by hijacking the reward system, a primitive neural circuit that evolved to drive behaviors necessary for survival and reproduction. All drugs of abuse are known to increase dopamine neurotransmission in mesolimbic reward areas, such as the ventral tegmental area and the nucleus accumbens (or ventral striatum). In a normally functioning reward system, when a hungry animal sees food, for example, dopamine levels increase to roughly 1.5-2X their resting levels in the nucleus accumbens to create a drive state that motivates the animal to pursue or move towards the food. When the food is actually eaten, the resulting increase in ß-endorphin levels in various reward areas, including the nucleus accumbens, is thought to confer a feeling of pleasure within the animal.[5] In a functional animal, or human being, the reward system is "connected" – that is, what is desired or craved creates a true feeling of pleasure, and what is desired most will generally be what is most critical to survival and reproductive prospects. Thus animals pursue behaviors beneficial to survival and reproduction because natural selection has evolved a system that supplies a biochemical reward – primarily ß-endorphin – whenever those behaviors are initiated or successfully completed.[6]

Drugs like cocaine and methamphetamine *directly* increase effective dopamine levels in the nucleus accumbens to roughly 10X their resting levels, in this case by inhibiting the function of the dopamine transporter.[7] Since these extremely high dopamine levels are a direct result of taking the drug, the reward system appears to interpret the association, at least at some level, as indicating that the drug has somehow become critical for survival. ✓ The relative levels of dopamine released into the reward system as a consequence of specific stimuli appear to determine the relative saliencies of those stimuli[8] – that is, the higher the dopamine levels, the more the reward system appears to interpret the stimuli, and an appropriate behavioral response to the stimuli, as being especially critical to survival or reproductive prospects. In drug addicts, reward circuits that respond both to the drug and to cues associated with the drug become strengthened, apparently through synaptic reinforcement mechanisms similar to those that occur during normal learning.[9] Drugs seem to become addictive, in other words, by tricking the mesolimbic reward circuit – which is primarily subcortical and appears to operate largely unconsciously – into behaving as if the drug had somehow become critical for survival. This is the unconscious illusion that appears to underlie every addiction.

When a drug like cocaine is first taken, it also typically releases large quantities of ß-endorphin, which various studies suggest creates the feeling of pleasure or euphoria that many drug users report. After prolonged use, however, as a true addiction begins to develop, the drug will gradually produce decreasing amounts of ß-endorphin.[10] The dopamine system, however, continues to be strongly sensitized in response to the drug. A number of studies, supporting the "incentive salience" model of addiction first proposed by Kent Berridge in 1993, suggest that dopamine surges create primarily a state of intense "wanting," or craving, distinct from a true feeling of pleasure, or "liking," which is mediated by ß-endorphin (or perhaps, in some cases, other endogenous opioids such as the enkephalins).[11] Addicts often admit that the limited amount of pleasure they derive from taking their drug does not justify its compulsive use.[12] This is the ultimate irony and tragedy of addiction: a drug that is intensely craved is not only ruinous to physical and emotional health, but also provides an ever-diminishing amount of pleasure to the addict. The reward system of the addict, therefore, becomes profoundly dysfunctional, or *disconnected*: the overwhelming dopamine-induced craving for the drug results in little, if any, real pleasure, and, furthermore, the pursuit and taking of the drug actually works *against* survival.

We suggest that addictions to various non-homeostatic states – such as anxiety, anger, regret, or self-pity – can create very similar disconnections in the reward system. Although these states typically are not consciously perceived as being pleasant, they have been shown, much like addictive drugs, to trigger a stress response that delivers significant quantities of both ß-endorphin and dopamine into reward areas. Because of the biochemical rewards they supply, these states can, we suggest, exert a dysfunctional pull on susceptible individuals.

Biochemical Rewards from Pain or Distress

Studies have shown that reward areas such as the nucleus accumbens are activated in human subjects who are, for example, engaging in sexual activity,[13] eating food,[14] looking at beautiful faces,[15] looking at humorous cartoons,[16] receiving money,[17] or listening to pleasing music.[18] But many other studies have shown that physical pain or emotional distress also trigger the release of dopamine and ß-endorphin into various reward areas.[19] Pinching the tail of a rat has been shown to release significant quantities of both ß-endorphin and dopamine into the nucleus accumbens.[20] Exposing rats to the urine odor of one of their natural predators, the fox, creates anxiety in the rat and also releases significant quantities of ß-endorphin into reward areas.[21] Brain imaging studies in humans have shown that sustained pain in a jaw muscle triggers the release of endogenous opioids into the nucleus accumbens and ventral tegmental area.[22] Large quantities of ß-endorphin are also released when self-mutilating human "cutters" cut themselves.[23] People with major depressive disorder have been shown to release ß-endorphin in their brains when they are asked to think of emotionally painful thoughts.[24] People who become particularly anxious before taking a stressful math test or giving a public speech release quantities of dopamine into reward areas that are in some cases comparable to the levels of dopamine released by cocaine or methamphetamine.[25] Noxious stimuli, such as mild burns or electric shocks, can produce increases of ß-endorphin in reward areas that are comparable to injections of a high dose of morphine.[26]

The release of endogenous opioids in response to physical injury probably evolved because of the analgesic, or pain-killing, properties of these opioids. In the wild, a physical injury is almost always a threat to survival, and often occurs in the context of a serious attack or other life-or-death circumstance. The analgesic properties of ß-endorphin allow animals or humans to focus on escaping the danger rather than immediately engaging in the defensive or recuperative postures that normally accompany sensations of extreme pain.[27] Thus natural selection appears to have evolved a strategy whereby injuries are primarily tended to after an emergency is over, when opioid levels typically decline and, consequently, the subjective experience of pain increases.

Dopamine levels also increase dramatically in any emergency situation,[28] probably for at least two reasons. First, studies suggest that dopamine release in reward areas in response to certain stimuli creates salience for those stimuli, focusing attention on them.[29] Second, dopamine is a key transmitter for initiating motor responses in the brain and thus would be a critical element of any emergency response.[30] In the ancestral environment, stimuli that indicated potential survival threats would also have often activated an emotional response prior to any physical encounter. Thus it makes evolutionary sense that stressors would activate an emotional response, even in the absence of a physical injury or physical interaction, that would stimulate the release of dopamine and ß-endorphin to prepare both for any motor responses that may be needed and for any physical injuries that may occur. A recent study by Susskind et al.[31] has suggested that the characteristic facial expressions associated with specific emotional states are designed to modify perceptual capacities in a manner appropriate to the stimuli that trigger the state. The wide-eyed facial expressions that accompany fear, for example, allow people to increase their effective visual fields, thus improving localization and tracking of potentially threatening stimuli. The authors suggest that emotional states such as fear are designed to enhance perception in preparation for potential action. Charles Darwin also repeatedly stressed that emotional states seem to have evolved primarily to mediate specific actions.[32]

Stressors activate two biological systems that are highly conserved in vertebrate animals: the SAM (sympatho-adreno-medullary) axis, and the HPA (hypothalamo-pituitary-adrenal) axis.[33] The SAM component of the stress response is responsible for the secretion of norepinephrine (or noradrenaline) and epinephrine (or adrenaline) into the bloodstream, which mediate, for example, the increased blood pressure and heart rate that are critical to any emergency response. The key effector in the HPA component of stress response is the glucocorticoid hormone cortisol, which mediates a wide variety of immune, cardiovascular, metabolic, and inflammatory changes also appropriate to an emergency response.[34] Both the HPA and the SAM axes are initially stimulated by the release of norepinephrine, which acts in the brain as an alarm response to any stressor. In the HPA axis, norepinephrine stimulates production of the hormone CRH in the hypothalamus, which triggers the synthesis of the protein precursor POMC. POMC, in turn, is processed into a number of protein products, including ß-endorphin and ACTH (or corticotropin). ACTH then triggers the release of cortisol by the adrenal cortex.[35] Thus the single protein precursor POMC, although it is differentially processed into various products in distinct regions of the brain,[36] contains both ACTH, which triggers the release of the prototypical stress hormone cortisol, and ß-endorphin, the key neurochemical that creates the feeling of pleasure or euphoria.

Noradrenaline, cortisol, and ß-endorphin are also strongly correlated with the release of dopamine, although the precise interactions between dopamine and the various stress hormones are complex.[37] It is very well established, however, that both dopamine and ß-endorphin, the key neuro-chemicals responsible for drug addiction and also for driving and rewarding the pursuit of natural rewards like sex and food, are released into reward areas as part of the normal stress response.[38] Stressful states, therefore, may be at least partially rewarding in that they appear to stimulate both the "wanting," dopamine-driven, element, and also the "liking," ß-endorphin-driven, element, of the reward system. The activation of both "wanting" and "liking" circuits by various stressors could therefore potentially lead to an addiction to both the stressors themselves and to the circumstances that may have created those stressors.

Emotional Pain and Physical Pain

As complex emotional states began to evolve in the earliest mammals about a hundred and fifty million years ago, the subjective experience of emotional pain appears to have been partially created by coopting the neural circuits that were already mediating the experience and response to *physical* pain – circuits that had already existed for hundreds of millions of years. Brain imaging studies have shown that experiences of emotional pain activate many of the same regions in the brain that are activated by physical pain.[39] Furthermore, opioids such as ß-endorphin appear to dull emotional pain as well as physical pain. For example, when mothers in various mammalian and avian species are unintentionally separated from their infants, the consequent separation distress is alleviated by opioid agonists.[40] Physical pain, therefore, and emotional pain or distress, appear to elicit very similar responses in the brain, at least partially through the activation of a stress response, and are similarly alleviated by opioids like ß-endorphin.

Cross-Sensitization between Stress and Addictive Drugs

A great deal of evidence suggests that stress and stress hormones cross-sensitize with addiction and addictive drugs – that is, exposure to stressors makes people or experimental animals more susceptible to addictive drugs, and addictive drugs make people or animals more susceptible to stress.[41] Stress and cocaine have been shown to elicit similar synaptic adaptations in dopamine neurons in reward areas.[42] Addictive drugs also appear to mediate many of their effects by themselves triggering an intense stress response.[43]

The people who are most susceptible to drug addiction, addictive behaviors, neuroses, and psychopathology appear to almost always have overactive stress systems. In most cases where dysfunction is apparent, resting cortisol levels are higher than average, but in others, such as with post-traumatic stress disorder (PTSD), resting cortisol levels can be *lower* than average. However, studies suggest that people with PTSD typically have chronically high levels of adrenaline, noradrenaline, and CRF, which are also associated with the stress response, and, furthermore, may have especially strong cortisol and ß-endorphin responses upon reactivation of their traumas.[44] Thus even in the absence of high resting cortisol levels, nearly all psychological dysfunctions appear to be associated with overactive stress systems.

Children who have been sexually or physically abused typically have hyperreactive stress responses and the hyperreactivity frequently lasts, to varying extents, into adulthood. In one study, adult women who had been abused as children and were suffering from major depressive disorder, had surges in levels of the stress hormone ACTH in response to a public speaking task that were about 6X higher than the ACTH response of controls.[45] Abused children also, according to several studies, have a far greater chance of becoming drug addicts or alcoholics than children who have not been abused, and are at far greater risk for developing various anxiety disorders as well as psychopathologies such as schizophrenia.[46] Monkey and rat infants who have been abused or severely stressed – for instance, by repeated social defeat stress or maternal separation – also tend to develop hyperreactive stress systems.[47] These animals, like abused and severely stressed children, also become significantly more prone to self-administering addictive drugs as adults.[48]

Drug addicts themselves typically have hyperreactive stress responses, and release dopamine and cortisol in response to stressors at levels that can be comparable to the levels released after cocaine or methamphetamine use.[49] When a recovering drug addict relapses, the relapse almost always comes about in one of three ways: the addict may be exposed to a trigger associated with the drug, such as walking past a previous "buy spot" for the drug; the addict may actually take a small amount of the drug, and this once again triggers compulsive use; or the addict may experience something that is particularly stressful, and the stressful state itself triggers compulsive drug use.[50] These behavioral findings are consistent with the notion that the stress hormones released by stressful states have very similar effects to those of addictive drugs.[51]

Exposure to severe stress in utero, in both humans and experimental animals, is also a significant risk factor for the development of both a hyperreactive stress system and drug addiction later in life.[52] Cortisol is known to cross the placenta from the bloodstream of the mother into the bloodstream of the fetus, and so when a mammalian mother experiences severe stress, the fetus will typically be exposed to elevated cortisol levels as well[53]. Prenatal exposure to drugs like cocaine similarly predispose the fetus to both a hyperreactive stress system and to developing a drug addiction later in life.[54]

Effects of Stress and Addictive Drugs on Dopamine Receptors

Severe stress and exposure to addictive drugs also have similar effects on dopamine receptor levels in reward areas. In group-living animals such as rats, baboons, and monkeys, the more submissive animals typically have higher stress and cortisol levels than the more dominant animals and also have fewer dopamine type-2 receptors (D_2 receptors) in reward areas.[55] The more submissive animals are also significantly more prone to self-administering addictive drugs than dominant animals.[56] Furthermore, all animals that chronically self-administer addictive drugs develop low D_2 receptor densities (or levels) that are comparable to the densities seen with submissive animals. Low D_2 receptor densities are also seen in individually housed animals, which, like submissive animals, become highly prone to self-administering addictive drugs.[57] Individual housing imposes a social isolation that acts as a stressor for any group-living animal, creating an extreme version of the social isolation typically found with low ranking animals, and particularly low ranking males, in various species.[58] When the animals are removed from individual housing and introduced back into a group, the animals that become more dominant show an increase in dopamine receptor levels, and a declining propensity to self-administer addictive drugs, while those that become submissive show low receptor densities similar to those seen with individually housed animals. In humans, alcoholics and people addicted to cocaine, methamphetamine, or opiates also have extremely low D_2 receptor densities in reward areas.[59]

Low dopamine receptor densities appear to be a response to chronically high levels of dopamine, whether those high dopamine levels are due to addictive drugs, high levels of stress, or other factors.[60] When dopamine levels become especially high, dopamine receptors apparently decline as a protection against excessive dopamine neurotransmission. Rats that, for purely genetic reasons, have especially high levels of motor activity in response to novel environments, or that score high on impulsivity tests, also have high levels of dopamine and low dopamine receptor densities, and are especially prone to compulsively self-administering addictive drugs.[61] Similarly, human studies have shown that people who are particularly impulsive and novelty-seeking report a more pleasant subjective response to addictive drugs, and are significantly more prone to drug addiction than individuals with lower ratings for impulsivity.[62]

Obese people also have chronically low dopamine receptor densities, and the greater their body mass index, the lower their dopamine receptor densities.[63] The process of feeding significantly increases dopamine concentrations, and researchers have speculated that, in obese individuals, dopamine receptor levels decline in response to the high dopamine levels that result from chronic, compulsive over-eating.[64] Studies have also shown that people with eating disorders are significantly more likely than controls to have undergone severe stress or abuse in early life, or to have been raised in severely dysfunctional family environments.[65]

Dopamine, Addiction, and Addictive Behavior

Mutant mice that are incapable of synthesizing dopamine become lethargic and listless, indicating that dopamine neurotransmission is critical for motivating the animals to seek food and to attend to salient stimuli in their environment.[66] People with low dopamine receptor levels, whether due to genetic or environmental causes, or both, may also require high levels of dopamine in reward areas to drive sufficient dopamine transmission to create motivated states. If their dopamine levels decline, they may become as listless as the dopamine-deficient mutant mice. Thus once dopamine receptor levels become low, high levels of dopamine apparently must be sustained to drive sufficient dopamine neurotransmission.

In humans, dopamine levels can be sustained at an elevated level in a number of ways. First, the stress system can be chronically overdriven by engaging in emotional states such as anxiety that activate a stress response and consequently elevate dopamine levels. Second, activities such as eating can be engaged in compulsively, which will also activate elements of the stress system and drive up dopamine levels.[67] Third, addictive drugs can be used. Healthy, homeostatic payoffs may also be capable of elevating dopamine to acceptable levels in the presence of low dopamine receptor densities, although the available evidence suggests that lasting states of homeostasis are probably associated with higher levels of dopamine receptors.

When food is intensely craved, the craving not only dramatically increases dopamine levels in reward areas, but can also produce more modest releases of ß-endorphin.[68] In this way, compulsive craving, which is typically associated with, for example, overeating, could elevate dopamine levels, driving dopamine neurotransmission, and could also drive the release of ß-endorphin. The act of eating will itself produce substantial releases of ß-endorphin, and probably more modest additional release of dopamine into reward areas.[69]

Taken as a whole, these data support a simple model of addiction and addictive behavior in humans. When dopamine receptor levels become low, which typically seems to occur as a consequence of prenatal or early life stress, certain individuals, particularly those who already have a genetic predisposition towards elevated dopamine levels,[70] can become prone to addiction of various types. Because any behavior that is emotionally or physically arousing will, by acting through the stress response, release both dopamine and ß-endorphin into reward areas, these behaviors may become necessary, or at least unconsciously *perceived* as being necessary, for creating acceptable dopamine and ß-endorphin levels in the reward system.

Stress and Neurotic Disorders, or "Emotional Addictions"

Neuroticism has been defined as the habitual tendency to experience distress and other negative affects.[71] Psychologists have frequently noted the element of self-abuse in neurotic behavior. Freud, for example, often spoke of the neurotic's self-tormenting drives,[72] and Adler suggested that "the whole arrangement of the neurosis follows the trait of self-torture."[73] We propose that all neuroses are driven by "emotional" addictions – that is, by addictions to negative or distressing emotional states such as anxiety, anger, regret, shame, or self-pity, in which people unconsciously engage in these states merely to derive the biochemical payoff that the states supply. If a person engages in any of these emotional states only occasionally, then that person is unlikely to have an addiction to those states. An emotional addiction is only indicated when specific negative emotional states are engaged in repeatedly and compulsively, particularly when there is often no plausible or functional reason for engaging in such a state. With an emotional addiction, the emotion is simply *used* to derive a biochemical payoff, although the process by which the emotion is, in effect, created or manufactured by the individual, is partly or wholly unconscious. Although it may seem counterintuitive that an unpleasant emotional state is somehow rewarding, and that such a state would be purposefully sought, we must recall that the reward system, and the mechanisms that generate "wanting" and "liking" within the reward system, appear to operate largely unconsciously.[74] Furthermore, such a notion appears to be entirely consistent with widely observed neurotic behaviors.

As with all other addictions, people become especially prone to emotional addictions when they are not deriving healthy biochemical payoffs from functional, homeostatic states, such as healthy play, fulfilling relationships, or meaningful work. It is almost as if an unconscious decision were made that if one cannot derive payoffs from being happy, or from engaging in pleasurable states or activities, one will have to derive those payoffs from negative emotional states. Thus people can become unconsciously driven to engineer circumstances that perpetuate certain negative emotional states.

Once a hyperreactive stress response is established, it probably *is* more difficult to both engage in homeostatic states and to derive sufficient payoffs from those states. The high dopamine levels that result from an overdriven stress system will create a decline in dopamine receptor levels, and then it may become more difficult to maintain sufficient dopamine neurotransmission from more modest natural rewards, such as moderate eating, or from small pleasures such as watching a beautiful sunset. The addictive loop can become further reinforced because negative emotional states – and non-homeostatic states in general – evolved largely to warn us about potential survival threats. Chronic anxiety will perpetuate the illusion that there is something to be anxious about, although the truth is likely to be that there is nothing imminent that represents a significant survival risk, and, furthermore, that the chronic anxiety is only increasing the chances that something unpleasant really *will* happen. And just as chronic use of addictive drugs is ruinous to health, compulsively and chronically engaging in negative emotional states drives the stress system excessively, and an overdriven stress system has been shown to significantly increase susceptibility to a number of medical conditions, including viral and bacterial infections, high blood pressure, and various autoimmune disorders.[75]

Studies suggest that people can indeed become unconsciously motivated to pursue biochemical rewards. In one double-blind experiment,[76] human subjects who had the option of receiving either a placebo, a low dose of methamphetamine, or a small amount of money, consistently chose the methamphetamine, even though they appeared to be entirely unconscious that the drug had a rewarding effect. We suggest that compulsive states of anxiety, for example, similarly supply a biochemical reward, even though the rewarding effects of such states may be entirely unconscious. The rewarding effects of a state such as anxiety may be doubly concealed, since the conscious perception or interpretation of negative emotional states is typically that the state itself is unpleasant.

A non-homeostatic state such as anxiety will, because of the stress response associated with the emotion, apparently always deliver a biochemical payoff, although that payoff may typically be unconscious. However, the state can be functional if it represents an alert to a true danger, and leads to a response that is geared towards overcoming or avoiding the danger, eventually allowing a return to homeostasis. It is only when such non-homeostatic states are engaged in purposefully and compulsively, if unconsciously, that true addictions to these states can develop.

Anxiety, Depression, and Emotional Addictions

Depressives are well known to have preferential access to painful thoughts, frequently ruminating about past events that stir feelings of humiliation, hurt, or regret.[77] Kennedy et al.[78] found that patients with major depression release significant amounts of endogenous opioids when they are asked to think of emotionally painful thoughts. We suggest that, for the depressive, such thoughts become a ready supply of biochemical payoffs. Depression and anxiety disorders are also very frequently comorbid – for example, up to 90% of people who have anxiety disorders will suffer from clinical depression at some point in their lives.[79] Anxiety has also been shown to release ß-endorphin and dopamine into reward areas, in some cases activating the reward system as intensely as addictive drugs like cocaine.[80] In humans and experimental animals, chronic stress, which typically accompanies chronic anxiety, also tends to create anhedonia, a defining feature of depression.[81]

The symptoms of depression are nearly identical to the symptoms that arise from withdrawal from addictive drugs. We suggest that people with depression typically have one or more strong emotional addictions, such as addictions to anxiety, regret, or shame. While the drug payoff is being received – for example during states of extreme anxiety or worry – the depression is temporarily kept at bay. But, partly because of the phenomenon of tolerance, where increasing amounts of a drug typically become required to achieve the same effect as the previous dose, if the process of compulsively and repeatedly engaging in such non-homeostatic states is allowed to continue indefinitely, the person may suffer serious health consequences, if not death itself. Thus the homeostatic drive will at some point exert itself, and ease the state of anxiety or worry, so that the stress system is not being so intensely overdriven. And when a brain that has become adapted to the biochemical payoffs that chronic anxiety supplies is suddenly no longer receiving those payoffs, a form of drug withdrawal will result, and such withdrawal, we propose, is typically associated with the lethargy and anhedonia that are defining features of depression. Brunton and Russell[82] similarly suggest that postpartum depression may be a consequence of the dramatic decline in cortisol levels following birth.

There is also now strong evidence suggesting that antidepressants such as fluoxetine (Prozac) mediate their antidepressant effects not primarily by increasing serotonin transmission, as was previously thought, but by stimulating neurogenesis and neuronal proliferation.[83] The most effective method of treating depression, electro-convulsive therapy (ECT), appears to massively disrupt previous neuronal connections and also strongly stimulate neurogenesis and neural proliferation.[84] On the other hand, chronic stress has been shown to greatly diminish neuronal plasticity in the brain, and typically leads to more stereotyped behaviors and thought patterns, and lower levels of mental flexibility.[85]

We suggest that antidepressants and ECT may be effective in alleviating depression, at least in part, because they disrupt dysfunctional neuronal pathways that have been strongly reinforced by addiction. These treatments then also stimulate the formation of new, more functional neuronal pathways. That is, because non-homeostatic states consistently deliver such significant biochemical payoffs, in depressive illnesses the pathways that are responsible for triggering and engendering such states have become fixed and ingrained, and those pathways must somehow be disrupted for the addictive loops associated with depression to be broken. It is only when these dysfunctional addictive pathways are disrupted, and new, more functional, neuronal pathways and circuits are formed and reinforced, that the depressive symptoms will substantially improve.

The Evolution and Function of the Stress Response

In the ancestral environment that shaped the evolution of our hunter-gatherer ancestors, non-homeostatic states such as anxiety were probably only experienced in response to true survival risks. Ultimately, anything that evolved to trigger a stress response seems to have pertained, at least in the ancestral environment, to survival. The so-called "stress response" appears to have evolved to engage during any form of motivated activity,[86] and was labeled as a "stress" response primarily because it was originally discovered as a baseline physiological response to noxious agents.[87] A stress response, however, occurs not only in response to stimuli indicating direct threats to survival, but also to stimuli that indicate the presence of opportunities that may enhance survival or reproductive prospects.[88] A risk to reproductive prospects is also, in essence, a risk to survival in the sense that it risks the survival of potential offspring and the genes that the offspring are vehicles for.[89] Animals and people are generally motivated to pursue attractive mates because attractiveness indicates vigorous health, and vigorous health indicates superior genes that will give rise to superior offspring with favorable chances of survival.[90] Therefore mating choices and opportunities are ultimately about survival as well. In this sense, the stress response might more appropriately be called the "survival" response.

The stress response is activated if, for example, a person is attacked by a wild animal, but it is also activated when the person feels strong desire for a potential sexual partner. In the ancestral environment, missing a favorable opportunity to form a stable relationship with, or have sex with, an especially favorable partner could have risked genetic death. This seems to be why we evolved to produce such a strong stress response under the circumstances of strong desire or craving. The stress response is similarly activated during the intense craving that comes from an opportunity to eat under the condition of extreme hunger.[91]

While the feeling of craving or desire appears to be primarily driven by dopamine release, the state of craving food, or the anticipation of eating food that may soon be available, has also been shown to release endogenous opiates.[92] Consequently, states of craving, like states of emotional distress, such as anxiety or regret, can also be purposefully, if unconsciously, *used* to dysfunctionally derive biochemical payoffs. States of extreme craving are also non-homeostatic states that, in the ancestral environment, generally indicated either a severe threat to survival or successful reproduction, or the risk of a high opportunity cost if the highlighted opportunity was not acted upon.

Food and Sex Addictions

Eating and sex, perhaps the two strongest natural reinforcers, should ideally be almost completely pleasurable, homeostatic activities, and they largely evolved to be such. But like any other activity or stimuli that create biochemical rewards, they become prone to addiction when they create unnecessary pain or distress. Any activity may sometimes produce *incidental*, unintended pain – such as an injury from a physical play activity, or emotional pain from a well-intended but failed love affair – but pain that is involved in addiction is pain that is purposefully, if unconsciously, *used* and perpetuated just to deliver the biochemical, or "drug," payoff that such pain supplies. Many addictions involve feelings that masquerade as being intensely pleasurable, but these supposedly pleasurable feelings are, in truth, mingled with a great deal of pain. Such is the case with food and sex addictions.

The key step in food and sex addiction is compulsive craving. When we compulsively crave an object or a person, we almost always have to unconsciously overvalue what is being craved – we have to lie to ourselves about how pleasurable or satisfying it will truly be to attain the object of desire, and we have to lie to ourselves about the repercussions of our actions and decisions, about the negative emotional states like anger, regret, and shame that will be a consequence of our actions. This is the precise dynamic that operates in a drug addiction. Many drug addicts admit that the state of craving a drug often produces a greater "high" than the actual taking of the drug, which is often anticlimactic.[93] Not long after the drug is taken, the "high" will very often become mingled with various negative affects. The only significant differences between drug addiction and food and sex addictions, in this sense, are first, that the object of craving is different, and second, that in a food or sex addiction the only harmful "drugs" are the biochemical payoffs derived from the stress response triggered by painful emotional states.

Compulsive craving leads us into poor, non-homeostatic choices – such as eating a gallon of ice cream or sleeping with our friend's spouse – that frequently lead to negative emotional states such as shame, guilt, or regret. The non-homeostatic choices are typically a consequence of a delusional over-valuing of the object of craving. The resulting out-of-balance, non-homeostatic states, which tend to be persistent, make it more difficult to engage in healthy, homeostatic states and to derive the functional payoffs that those states supply. This is the cycle of addiction. Because food and sex are necessary for survival and well-being, food and sex addictions can be especially insidious, and can be easy for the addict to falsely, and therefore dysfunctionally, justify. But like any other addiction, such addictions only perpetuate painful states.

While excessive eating produces large quantities of dopamine and ß-endorphin, anorexia, apparently through chronic activation of a stress response, also produces large payoffs.[94] In the wild, a state of starvation often stimulates a dopamine-driven desire to search for food, which probably also results in the release of at least small quantities of ß-endorphin. With eating disorders, decisions about what to eat and when to eat also become a constant emotionally arousing "drama," which will also trigger a stress response and create dysfunctional biochemical payoffs. All of these elements, because they perpetuate states of non-homeostasis that are interpreted by the brain as signaling a survival emergency, make it increasingly difficult to derive healthy, homeostatic payoffs, and this dynamic perpetuates the addictive cycle.

Homeostatic eating or sex involve an honest assessment of what is desired and why it is desired, an honest assessment about how we are likely to feel after the specific acts of eating or having sex, and a true enjoyment, in the moment, of the actual acts. Although addiction creates the illusion that it enhances the pleasure of activities like eating and having sex, addiction actually corrupts or ruins the profound pleasures and joys that can be derived from these behaviors.

People in modern industrialized cultures are particularly prone, for instance, to food addictions, at least in part, because foods rich in sugars and fats, which are often physiologically desirable and also release large quantities of ß-endorphin in reward areas,[95] were rare or nonexistent in the ancestral environment, but are widespread, and also aggressively advertised, in the modern world. Humans are not well-equipped, either psychologically or physically, to eat such foods, particularly in immoderate amounts, and a diet containing significant amounts of such foods tends to be both psychologically and physically non-homeostatic. However, even rich foods can be eaten homeostatically if the following conditions apply: if they are eaten without self-delusion about their true effects; if they are eaten consciously and not compulsively; and if they don't cause or perpetuate negative affects. There is a great deal of evidence suggesting that the development of eating disorders is strongly associated with severe stress in early childhood.[96] We suggest that food addictions develop in the same way as emotional addictions and drug addictions, which are also strongly associated with prenatal or childhood stress and with the development of a hyperreactive stress response.[97]

Emotional Addictions as a Gateway to Other Addictions

The development of a hyperreactive stress system appears to increase the risk of all types of addiction for two primary reasons. First, the more hyperreactive the stress response, the greater, in general, the biochemical payoff will be whenever the stress response is activated during a non-homeostatic state. Second, an overdriven stress response will keep a person in a nearly chronic state of non-homeostasis, and the more one engages in such non-homeostatic states, particularly when large biochemical payoffs are being derived from those states, the more difficult it becomes to transition back to homeostasis, and to derive healthy payoffs from homeostatic states. And the longer one remains in non-homeostasis, particularly when such states are *not*, in reality, necessary for survival, the more the illusion becomes reinforced that these states are engaged in because survival is somehow at stake, and the more severe the addiction becomes.

Because emotional addictions and drug addictions both typically depend on a hyperreactive stress response for their expression, any circumstance or dynamic that increases the risk for the development of emotional addictions will also increase the risk for the development of drug addiction and alcoholism. And since emotional addictions, or addictions to non-homeostatic states, will tend to perpetuate the engagement in non-homeostatic states, a child who succumbs to emotional addictions will spend more time in non-homeostasis and be at further risk for more serious addictions in the future, such as drug addiction and alcoholism. Just as attachment researchers and many other psychologists have long suggested that the development of neurotic behavior and other dysfunctions begins in early childhood,[98] we similarly suggest that addiction to non-homeostatic states typically begins in infancy or early childhood, and sets the stage for the development of other, often more serious, addictions. Since drugs and alcohol are rarely available during infancy, we suggest that the true "gateway" drugs that can lead to drug addiction and alcoholism are typically the stress hormones that are dysfunctionally delivered by emotional addictions.

The Stress Response and Parenting

Although abuse, parental loss, or other severe stressors during childhood create the greatest risk for the development of a hyperreactive stress response, the stress system is also clearly influenced by more subtle aspects of the parent-child relationship. Attachment researchers have shown that infants who are securely attached, who seem to have healthy, loving relationships with their parents, generally have lower cortisol levels, and also have more moderate cortisol responses to stressors. Infants who are insecurely attached have cortisol levels that are generally higher, and their cortisol responses to stressors tend to be both exaggerated and prolonged.[99]

The key element in rearing secure infants is thought to be sensitivity and attunement to the infants' needs, and, more specifically, the ability of parents to regulate the negative emotions of their infants[100] – or, in our terminology, to help the infants come back into homeostasis if they become distressed or immersed in a non-homeostatic state. Infants are effectively brought back into homeostasis only when their true needs are appropriately addressed – and, to infants, all needs are instinctively perceived as survival needs.

To an infant, for example, *attention* from the mother and other care-givers is perceived as a survival need. One of the key predictors of survival in all mammals, and particularly in primates, is the extent of maternal commitment,[101] and attention is a strong indicator of such commitment. John Bowlby, the father of attachment theory, suggested that "the young child's hunger for his mother's love and presence is as great as his hunger for food."[102] Numerous studies have shown that when maternal commitment or attention is inconstant or unreliable, such as when a mother is clinically depressed, it is extremely distressing to the infant, significantly raising cortisol levels.[103]

When an infant's needs for food, warmth, attention, or comfort, for example, are not sufficiently addressed, the infant will spend a great deal of time in non-homeostasis, and will become at grave risk for developing addictions to various non-homeostatic states. Furthermore, such a pattern can create a dysfunctional dynamic with the mother when the frightened infant begins to act in certain ways to attract the mother's attention in an effort to have perceived survival needs met. For instance, infants may become overly focused on their *mother's* emotional state, rather than on their own. This type of dynamic, along with other, more serious, traumas, such as overt abuse, may lead infants and children to become disconnected from their own emotional states. Such disconnections are apparent in a wide variety of dysfunctions. For example, one study concluded that anorexics are far more likely than controls to be alexithymic – that is, to have great difficulty in recognizing and categorizing their feelings or emotional states.[104] More severe forms of disconnection from one's own emotional state have been widely reported as a consequence of severe traumas such as physical or sexual abuse.[105]

Michael Meaney and his colleagues have clearly shown how parenting behavior can affect the stress response in rats.[106] Rat pups with mothers who frequently lick and groom them have a significantly lower response to stressors than do pups whose mothers lick and groom them less. Cross-fostering experiments indicate that these specific effects on the stress response are not significantly influenced by genetic factors in this case, but rather are determined causally by the type of maternal care the pups receive. Rat pups that receive low levels of maternal care are also significantly more prone to self-administering addictive drugs than are pups who receive high levels of maternal care.[107] These studies appear to correspond closely with similar findings in monkeys and other mammals, and may have identified a general dynamic in the development of the stress system in all mammals.[108]

Human studies, although more indirect, suggest a similar dynamic. College students who report the most distant and troubled relationships with their parents – presumably reflecting insecure attachment – have been shown to respond to stressful math tests and public speaking tasks with exaggerated cortisol responses, and with dopamine surges in reward areas that can be up to 3X stronger than those of students reporting close and loving parental relationships. In some cases, these dopamine surges can be equivalent to the dopamine surges seen in response to cocaine or methamphetamine.[109]

It has been suggested that parenting behavior in various species molds the stress system of the infant in a way that will optimize the infant's chances of surviving in specific environmental circumstances.[110] Parenting behavior is proposed as being both an expression of current environmental circumstances and a predictor of future environmental circumstances. Thus in difficult circumstances, such as drought or persistent danger from predators or hostile conspecifics, levels of maternal care tend to be lower, triggering a hyperreactive stress response in the infant, which, under these environmental circumstances, is thought to be adaptive. In more favorable circumstances, when a more moderate stress response is likely to be adaptive, levels of maternal care tend to be higher.

In many species, including humans, the level of maternal anxiety appears to be a critical determinant of the level of maternal care. An anxious mother will generally be significantly less attentive to her infant's needs and will provide a lower level of care than a relaxed mother.[111] For wild animals and human hunter-gatherers, chronic anxiety in the mother will almost always reflect environmental conditions that are perilous for survival prospects, circumstances under which the development of a hyperreactive stress response in infants would probably be adaptive. However, in modern industrialized societies, maternal anxiety is far more often the result of a maladaptive neurosis rather than an emotional response that reflects the actual environmental conditions and the true level of the associated survival risks. The mother's anxiety in this case would, in our terminology, reflect an emotional addiction to anxiety. And because an anxious mother will generally provide a lower level of care, the mother will often, in effect, pass on her maladaptive addiction to anxiety to her infant. Studies have suggested that the emotional responses of human infants, in particular, are exquisitely sensitive to levels of anxiety in their mothers.[112]

Chronically overdriven stress responses conditioned by maternal behavior may be perpetuated by epigenetic changes in genes that are involved in the stress response. Meaney and his colleagues have identified hundreds of genes in the rat, such as the glucocorticoid receptor (the receptor for cortisol, or corticosterone), that may be altered epigenetically by low levels of maternal care.[113] Emerging evidence also suggests that the altered patterns of gene expression seen in drug addiction may be perpetuated by specific epigenetic changes, and that these changes may remain relatively stable for months or years in recovering addicts, elevating the risk of relapse.[114] Many of the epigenetic changes found in addicts are likely to also perpetuate a hyperreactive stress response.

The main role of genetics in affecting the development of a hyperreactive stress response may well be in influencing how infants *respond* to relatively inattentive parenting, or to severe stress or abuse. Caspi et al.[115] showed that if children have an especially active genetic variant for MAOA, a molecule that degrades dopamine and noradrenaline following their release, the children are protected from the most severe psychological effects of abuse. Since both dopamine and noradrenaline are critical elements of the stress response, this genetic variant, and other specific variants that influence the stress response, may create a protective effect by moderating the stress response in reaction to severe stress, abuse, or low levels of parental care. The presence of these genetic variants may explain, at least in part, why a significant subset of people never develop severe neuroses or psychopathologies despite extensive childhood sexual or physical abuse.[116]

Low Status and Addiction

Another attribute that is clearly associated with a hyperreactive stress system and various kinds of addiction is low status. All group-living animals have some form of dominance hierarchy, and in most mammals, including rats, monkeys, and baboons, the animals lowest in the hierarchy have the highest levels of cortisol, and usually appear to be more anxious than the dominant animals.[117] Low ranking animals are also far more prone to self-administering addictive drugs under experimental conditions than are high ranking animals.[118]

Although status in humans is far more complicated than it is in any other animal, a number of lines of evidence suggest that the same dynamic operates in human cultures. A number of studies have shown that people at the lowest socioeconomic levels tend to have significantly higher cortisol levels than people at higher socioeconomic levels.[119] Children as young as six years old who live in poorer homes have far higher cortisol levels than do children of the same age who live in wealthier homes.[120] And although the contributing factors are probably numerous and complex, people from the lowest socioeconomic levels also clearly have a far greater risk of abusing drugs and alcohol than do people at higher socioeconomic levels.[121]

Other less severe status differences also appear to affect cortisol levels in humans. In one study, for example, when cortisol measurements from members of a college tennis team were taken throughout the season, the lowest seeded players tended to have the highest cortisol levels. When formerly top-seeded players dropped into the lower seeds, their cortisol levels tended to increase.[122]

In humans, low socioeconomic status seems to be very frequently internalized as low self-esteem, especially in young children, and low self-esteem is a key indicator of a low degree of psychological well-being.[123] In addition, poverty often acts as a severe stressor for a family, and thus low socioeconomic status is often associated with low levels of parental care and high levels of family dysfunction, putting children at further risk for the development of hyperreactive stress responses and later substance abuse.[124]

Many psychologists, including Sigmund Freud, Alfred Adler, and Karen Horney,[125] have suggested that a strong correlation exists between low self-esteem and neurotic behavior. Feelings of low self-esteem in many cases correlate with low objective levels of status, but in many other cases represent internalized, *subjective* determinations of status that can often be wildly distorted. Many studies have suggested that low levels of parental care, or high levels of family dysfunction, even in relatively wealthy homes, increase the risk of a child developing low self-esteem.[126] The extremely low levels of self-esteem typically found in substance abusers is probably both a predis-posing factor that leads to substance abuse, and also a further consequence of such abuse.[127]

Hunter-Gatherer vs. Post-Agricultural Environments

A key element of our model is that the radical differences between modern environmental circumstances and the circumstances under which humans evolved as hunter-gatherers tend to create a driving force towards addictive behavior in modern environments. It has become increasingly well accepted that the human brain and human behavior were shaped by the environmental context of hunter-gatherer life.[128] Until about 12,000 years ago, when agricultural methods were invented and began to spread, all humans and pre-humans lived as hunter-gatherers, and had done so for millions of years. Although some genetic changes have occurred since the invention of agriculture, those changes appear to have been relatively superficial.[129] It seems highly unlikely, moreover, that there have been significant changes during this period in the structure and function of the reward system, the stress system, or other neural circuits involved in the genesis and maintenance of addiction. Many of these structures and systems are shared among all mammals and are thus evolutionarily ancient, while others were refined during the millions of years during which our human and pre-human ancestors lived as hunter-gatherers.

Contemporary hunter-gatherers, such as the !Kung of the Kalahari Desert or the Ache of Paraguay, provide the best available models for the circumstances that were likely to have been faced by our hunter-gatherer ancestors.[130] Although distinct variations exist between contemporary hunter-gatherer groups, both in the environmental circumstances they face and in their typical modes of behavior and interaction, a number of features that are relevant to our model appear to be nearly universal among hunter-gatherers. First, physical and sexual abuse of children – which is shockingly prevalent in many modern industrialized cultures, including the U.S. – is, by several accounts, extremely rare in hunter-gatherer societies.[131] Second, social isolation, which is very common in modern cultures, is essentially non-existent in hunter-gatherer bands, whose members tend to be tightly connected, both physically and emotionally.[132] In modern life, social isolation is particularly common in people who have been abused as children or have had dysfunctional upbringings.[133] Such isolation has been shown to raise cortisol levels[134] and is a well-established risk factor for the development of addictive and neurotic behaviors.[135] Third, a host of studies suggest that parenting behavior in technologically advanced cultures tends to be radically different from the typical parenting behavior found in hunter-gatherers, and is generally far less nurturing. For example, hunter-gatherer mothers generally respond to their infants' cries far more readily and effectively than do contemporary American mothers, and generally seem not only more attuned to the needs of their infants, but more attentive in addressing those needs.[136] Fourth, the status dynamics of hunter-gatherer bands are far more egalitarian than they are in post-agricultural societies, which are notably hierarchical,[137] Fifth, hunter-gatherers, partly because they are constantly surrounded by the natural world, are primarily oriented in the present moment,[138] a tendency that tends to be protective against addictive behavior.

Although there are clear status differences within hunter-gatherer bands, particularly among men, these differences tend to be far more subtle than the status differences found in modern cultures. The most notable status difference among hunter-gatherer men is that the highest status men, usually the best hunters or spiritual healers (shamans), often have multiple wives and also engage in a higher number of extramarital affairs.[139] However, in nearly every other sense, hunter-gatherer bands are far more egalitarian than modern cultures. Food, particularly large kills of meat, is almost universally shared, with meticulous care, among the individuals in the band.[140] Power is also generally distributed equally. While some individuals – usually older men – may be especially respected within the group and may have leadership roles, their power is very limited. By nearly all accounts, all important decisions in hunter-gatherer bands, which usually consist of about 25-50 people, are made with the input and consent of most of the band's adult members. If any man with especially high status becomes imperious or arrogant, he will quickly lose the band's respect and his influence will be greatly diminished.[141] The status of women among hunter-gatherers is probably also higher than it is in any other known culture.[142]

Since nearly all hunter-gatherer bands are nomadic or semi-nomadic, they generally have very few material possessions, and so material possessions are rarely the basis for status distinctions.[143] The development of agriculture and animal husbandry allowed groups of people to establish permanent settlements, which enabled the accumulation of possessions – ranging from decorative items to livestock animals – that began to act, at least in part, as status symbols. Permanent settlements also led to the establishment of governments and militaries with access to specialized weapons that gave some individuals infinitely more power than anyone could ever possibly achieve in a hunter-gatherer band.[144]

A great deal of evidence suggests that human beings are far more prone to various psychological disorders when they feel they are "beneath" other people, or when they feel they have little control over the circumstances of their lives.[145] No animal likes to be in the lower reaches of the status hierarchy, but for human beings, who have a long evolutionary history of relative egalitarianism and autonomy, being low in a hierarchy with extreme dichotomies in wealth and power seems to be especially stressful and unpleasant. Fehr, Bernhard, and Rockenbach[146] have shown that egalitarian preferences are strongly developed in children by the ages of seven to eight, suggesting that human egalitarianism has deep developmental and evolutionary roots. Other studies have indicated that adults also have strong egalitarian preferences.[147]

A critical element of our model is that feelings of being somehow "less than" other people is a major driving force, and perhaps *the* major driving force, in the development of addiction and addictive behavior. Chronic feelings of "less than" repeatedly trigger states of non-homeostasis. In our hunter-gatherer ancestors, having status that was significantly lower than other members of the band could be perilous for at least two reasons. First, people with especially low status would be at greatly increased risk of being thrown out of, or abandoned by, the band. And in the wild, human beings who are alone, especially without modern weaponry, have dramatically lower chances of surviving and reproducing. Second, low status levels, particularly for men, may drastically reduce, or even eradicate, potential mating opportunities. Both of these prospects are highly stressful, because, in the ancestral environment, they could have resulted in either literal death or genetic (reproductive) death. Furthermore, higher levels of status, particularly for men, increase the chances of finding a mate with superior genes who will be more likely to give birth to and rear a child who will also survive.[148]

In modern industrialized cultures, even people with very low relative status may not face any truly serious survival risk, particularly in countries with universal health care and adequate social services. And yet, we suggest, low status levels in modern life often trigger an unconscious stress response that reflects human evolutionary history. If the exceptionally low relative status levels often found in modern life were experienced within the context of a hunter-gatherer band, it would indicate an extremely dire risk to survival and reproduction. Although the same risks, at least in a relative sense, are generally not present in modern life, the same primitive emotional response is very frequently triggered.

Because gains in status are so favorable to survival prospects, human beings evolved to experience a gain in status as being pleasurable, and such status gains have been shown in a recent study to strongly activate reward areas.[149] But the same study also shows that a *loss* of status activates reward areas in the brain. Loss of status probably activates reward areas for the same reasons that various kinds of physical or emotional pain activate the reward system – because in the context of hunter-gatherer life, a severe loss of status may represent a true survival threat, and consequently will activate a stress response. Because loss of status, like physical and emotional pain, activates reward areas, yet another type of dysfunctional biochemical payoff becomes possible. The syndromes of people appearing to derive masochistic satisfaction from feeling "less than" other people, or of people who appear to unconsciously sabotage their prospects for raising their status or self-esteem, are well-known to psychotherapists.[150] Thus we suggest that the feeling of "less than" can itself become an addiction, as well as being a frequent trigger that leads into other addictions and addictive behaviors by creating a lingering state of non-homeostasis.

Child-rearing in Hunter-gatherer,
Agricultural, and post-Agricultural Cultures

Although child-rearing methods differ somewhat between different hunter-gatherer groups, a general pattern has emerged that appears to reflect nearly universal attributes of child-rearing among hunter-gatherers.[151] First, infants receive round-the-clock, on-demand nursing for at least two to three years, and often for four years. Second, during this period, the infant is rarely apart from the mother, and always sleeps directly next to the mother. Third, the infant receives an enormous amount of attention from both the parents and the rest of the band, many of whom are relatives of the infant. Fourth, the mother is extremely attentive to the infant – the focus is rarely on controlling the infant's behavior, but rather on responding to the infant's specific needs. Fifth, after weaning, and especially after the ages of about six to eight, the child becomes increasingly independent, and the parents and other band members encourage the child to be as self-sufficient as possible.[152]

Patterns of child-rearing change dramatically with the adoption of agriculture. Fouts et al.[153] found that Bofi farmers have markedly different child-rearing styles than Bofi hunter-gatherers, even though the two groups are very closely related culturally. In the Bofi farmers, mothers are not as attentive to their infants' needs, and infants are weaned relatively early, often with coercive methods that instill fear in the child. In Bofi farmers, the amount and quality of care from caregivers after weaning declines far more dramatically than it does with Bofi hunter-gatherers. The Bofi farmers physically hold their children about five times less than Bofi hunter-gatherers do, and also make more attempts to control the behavior of their children, with far less respect for the children's personal autonomy.[154]

In modern industrialized cultures, the divergence from hunter-gatherer child-rearing methods is in many ways even more stark. Frequent practices such as allowing an infant to cry for extended periods while alone in a room at night are likely to be traumatic for the infant.[155] Studies have also indicated that American mothers, for example, do not respond as readily or effectively to their infants' crying episodes as do hunter-gatherer mothers.[156] The ethos among many modern parents is try to control the behavior of their infants, or in effect to train the infant, rather than focusing on addressing the infant's needs. On the other hand, older children are frequently overprotected, and often don't develop the sense of self-sufficiency or competency that is critical to the growth of healthy self-esteem.[157] The nuclear family, which is typically the focus of family life in industrialized cultures, also creates a dense psychological environment that is far less forgiving of parental flaws than the extended kin and social groups found in hunter-gatherer bands.[158] In a real sense, it is nearly impossible for modern parents, particularly within the context of the nuclear family, to match the level of attention and care that hunter-gatherer bands, with their extended families and kin groups, typically supply their infants and children – and yet this is presumably the level of care that human infants have evolved to anticipate. It seems notable that many current child-rearing recommendations, such as those of attachment researchers, appear to be converging on the style of parenting found among hunter-gatherers.[159] Similarly, nutritional recommendations are largely converging on the typical hunter-gatherer dietary patterns.[160]

Most relevant to our model, many studies have shown that the failure to adequately address an infant's needs can be extremely stressful for the infant, creating persistent states of non-homeostasis. In hunter-gatherers, persistent states of non-homeostasis in the infant are probably a sign of extreme environmental or physiological peril. Relatively inattentive parenting would probably be a reflection of persistent anxiety in the mother,[161] which would probably in turn be a reflection of either poor social support within the band, unreliable sources of food, or persistent threats from predators or other people.[162] Any one of these conditions would represent a true survival threat to the mother and her infant, reflected in the mother's chronic anxiety.

Post-traumatic Stress Disorder, the
Repetition Compulsion, and Addiction

Freud devised the notion of the "repetition compulsion", or the "compulsion to repeat", to explain the behavior of many of his patients, whom he believed unconsciously sought to recover and repeat painful childhood emotional states and circumstances.[163] We suggest that the repetition compulsion is driven by biochemical addiction. Childhood traumas create non-homeostatic states that can deliver enormous biochemical payoffs. Such traumas can act, in effect, as a "drug" exposure, and can continue to exert a dysfunctional pull on the individual. If the child, or the adult the child becomes, is for any reason blocked from experiencing homeostatic states and deriving biochemical payoffs from those states, the trauma, and the negative emotional states associated with the trauma, will continue to exert a dysfunctional pull. For example, if a child is continually shamed or insulted by the parents, there is a significant risk that the child will unconsciously continue to seek these negative emotional states in various other circumstances.

The clearest example of a repetition compulsion is found in post-traumatic stress disorder (PTSD). In an important predecessor to our model, Bessel van der Kolk and Michael Greenberg proposed in 1987[164] that war veterans with PTSD can become "addicted to trauma," and may be unconsciously driven to re-engage in and relive their traumas in order to derive an endorphin reward, much like "cutters" derive the same reward by cutting themselves. Van der Kolk, Greenberg and their colleagues[165] also found that war veterans whose traumas were reactivated released significant quantities of ß-endorphin into their bloodstreams.

Relationship Dramas

Dysfunctional relationship "dramas" are an extremely common manifestation of emotional addiction. In relationship dramas, the participants are dysfunctionally, compulsively, and usually unconsciously, driven into non-homeostatic states so that they can derive biochemical payoffs from those states. The healthiest relationships have no unnecessary drama, and the relationship ideally helps to bring both participants back into homeostasis when they become distressed or out-of-balance. The individuals involved in relationship dramas typically have specific dysfunctional roles that are usually acquired early in childhood. We will describe the dynamics of such relationship dramas in detail elsewhere.

The participants in such dramas unconsciously seek partners who will trigger childhood dysfunctions and traumas, thus providing dysfunctional payoffs. Because the payoffs released from such dramas can be substantial, and can become mingled with sexual attraction, the dramas often masquerade as love, even when the relationship is dominated by negative mood states in both participants, or contains overt emotional or physical abuse.

The "Sadistic" Impulse and Addiction

Nearly all of us, at least under some circumstances, appear to be capable of deriving satisfaction, or a biochemical payoff, from another person's pain, particularly when we believe that the person has acted unethically or has done some sort of harm to us or to someone we care about. Studies involving games where money is exchanged between two players according to specified rules and agreements, have shown that neutral observers express satisfaction when players who act unfairly or unethically receive electric shocks.[166] Whether the observers are watching such punishment, or are themselves administering the punishment, reward areas in the brain become strongly activated, especially in those observers who express a strong desire for revenge.[167]

Any behavior or physical or emotional state that provides a significant biochemical payoff to the reward system is prone to addiction. But if a person is only acting in self-defense, or out of an authentic survival instinct, such as hunting animals for food or fending off an attack, biochemical payoffs from the pain of other people or animals will not become addictive. Unnecessary pain caused to other people or animals, however, is typically non-homeostatic. Part of the self knows that the pain inflicted was unnecessary, and the person inflicting that pain may, for example, feel shame, regret, and other negative emotions that are similar to those often felt after compulsive drug use, or compulsive shopping, gambling, or eating. Thus the sadistic impulse can lead people into addiction when it drives them away from homeostasis.

Because emotional pain and physical pain are processed so similarly in the brain, the sadistic impulse, at least in contemporary cultures, is probably most frequently manifested as a desire to harm others emotionally, rather than physically. Humans evolved to derive a biochemical payoff from injuring others emotionally for at least two reasons: first, as a means of self-defense to fend off emotional or physical attacks from other people; second, as a means of status enhancement, or a means of "defeating" or subduing a rival, or dropping them lower in the status hierarchy. But people who unnecessarily injure others emotionally, especially when the victims are children or other people who are relatively powerless, are engaging in a non-homeostatic drive that will only lead to addiction and further pain.

Mental Time Travel, Theory of Mind, and Addiction

The most recently evolved human capacities, such as "mental time travel" and "theory of mind," appear to be particularly prone to addiction. Although these two capacities may be present to a more limited extent in other primates, and perhaps some other animals,[168] they are far more elaborated in humans, and are also critical to nearly every addiction found in humans.

Mental time travel allows us to project ourselves into the past or the imagined future so that we not only derive an image of an event or circumstance in the past or the future, but can also access emotional states associated with those projections.[169] Mental time travel, which may have evolved in the human lineage as recently as 1.6 million years ago,[170] thus creates almost infinite possibilities for emotional addictions. Depressives, for example, very frequently project themselves into the past to recall painful episodes that trigger an emotional response. Kennedy et al.[171] showed that when depressives think an emotionally painful thought, their brains release endogenous opiates. With mental time travel, a dysfunctional payoff is always readily available. For instance, we can at any time conjure a memory, or an imaginative reconstruction of the past, that creates negative affects such as pain, regret, or shame. We can also at any time conjure an image of the future that creates anxiety. All of these products of mental time travel will generate dysfunctional payoffs.

But mental time travel is also one of our greatest gifts, integral to the human imagination and to creativity. In general, mental time travel only becomes dysfunctional if one or more of the following are operative: first, if it involves an illusion, a lie that we tell to ourselves; second, if it becomes compulsive – that is, a way of unconsciously, and in a sense involuntarily, deriving a biochemical payoff; third, if it is either overtly based on deriving a payoff from pain, or on deriving a payoff from a memory or craving that is mingled with pain; fourth, if it takes us unnecessarily out of the present moment and out of homeostasis, from which all of the healthiest and most functional biochemical payoffs are derived.

Similarly, theory of mind, which allows us to "project" mental states onto other people, animals, or even inanimate objects, is responsible for both the most profound and delightful human gifts and capacities, and also for some of the most severe human dysfunctions. Other animals, particularly chimpanzees and other great apes, clearly have some theory of mind capacities, but those capacities are far less developed than they are in humans.[172] In a hunter-gatherer context, theory of mind capacities have obvious adaptive value. For example, the capacity can be used to discern the mental states of potential mates, collaborators, or rivals within the band, or of people outside the band who may be plotting attack or other harm.[173] Theory of mind capacities are also useful for hunting, when the hunter is trying to discern the intentions and mental state of the prey. For example, hunters in hunter-gatherer bands often study an animal's tracks to determine whether the animal is tired or injured, and attempt to discern how the animal might behave when in these specific physical states.[174] These hunting skills depend heavily on theory of mind capacities.

Psychotherapists know only too well how false projections, which were enabled when theory of mind capacities evolved, can both lead to and perpetuate dysfunction.[175] While accurate projections have enormous adaptive value, the capacity for projection can also create remarkable illusions. We may feel we "know" what another person is thinking or feeling, and be entirely wrong. Projections appear to profoundly affect not only all of our relationships with other people, but our relationship to the world around us, as unconscious contents from the self are almost constantly being projected outward into the world.[176] Projection can enable deep compassion for and understanding of others, but can also lead to profoundly insidious dysfunctions.

Most types of emotional addiction would be impossible without mental time travel and theory of mind capacities, which can intermingle in powerful ways. Indeed, nearly every dysfunction discussed in this paper depends on both of these capacities. For example, we may derive a significant dysfunctional payoff from recalling a past event in which we were hurt emotionally by someone. But we can derive an even *greater* payoff if we project certain intentions onto that person – for instance, that this person regards us as inferior or unimportant, or consciously and purposefully intended to harm us, even though these projections may be grossly distorted or entirely inaccurate. Then we can derive a payoff not only from the emotional hurt, but also from the enhanced anger that the projection facilitates, or enhanced feelings or "less than." Although we can potentially project almost *anything* onto other people, the projection typically must be at least somewhat plausible, or the functional, homeostatic part of ourselves will too easily see through the unconscious ruse.

We propose that, at least in modern life, nearly all false projections, particularly those that create or engender negative affects, are driven by biochemical addiction. That is, when a person falsely projects intentions or beliefs onto other people or animals, those projections almost always act in the service of that person's own specific addictions.

This type of dysfunction is clearly illustrated by the fictional character Ahab in the novel *Moby-Dick*.[177] Ahab becomes obsessed with pursuing and killing the whale Moby-Dick, projecting all the world's malevolence onto an animal that is only trying to defend itself against men who are trying to kill it! Ahab's obsession creates a nearly continual dysfunctional payoff, arousing a blood lust to kill the whale, and an intense, wholly irrational anger directed towards the animal. The absurd and pathological projections onto Moby-Dick are acting to feed several of Ahab's various addictions, such as his addiction to irrational anger.

Sleep, Dreams, and Addiction

The urge to sleep, much like the urge to eat, is under strong homeo-static control. If we miss a night of sleep, a "hunger" for sleep will develop, and, when we do finally sleep, there will be a sleep "rebound," in which the amount or intensity of sleep will be increased.[178] Rats chronically deprived of sleep die in about the same number of days as they would if deprived of food.[179] Sleep may also be the purest natural state of homeostasis, in addition to having a more complicated and integral role in the maintenance of homeostasis. A recent study has suggested that sleep may be necessary for restoring synaptic homeostasis in neural circuits, showing that while wakefulness is associated with a net increase in synaptic strength in the cortex, sleep may redress this potential imbalance by mediating a net decrease in overall synaptic strength.[180] Thus sleep may be critical for the maintenance of homeostasis, and may also itself represent a state of homeo-stasis.

Addiction, which in our model represents the dysfunctional drive to *non*-homeostasis, can disrupt the homeostatic function of sleep in several ways. Most simply, all addictions can greatly diminish the total amount of time spent sleeping. An addiction to anxiety, for example, will continually drive the stress system, triggering the release of epinephrine, norepinephrine, and cortisol, which mimic the effect of stimulants such as amphetamine and can strongly interfere with both sleep onset and duration. As with all addictive patterns, a vicious cycle can develop where insufficient sleep further drives the stress response, and an overdriven stress response further impairs sleep.

Various studies suggest that an insufficient quantity of sleep can also be a critical trigger for various psychopathologies. It has been suggested, for example, that the key trigger for the manic phase in bipolar disorder may be disturbed sleep.[181] Disrupted sleep patterns are also strongly associated with many other neuroses and psychopathologies.[182] In the context of our model, disturbed sleep is both a cause and consequence of the states of non-homeostasis that are associated with neuroses and psychopathologies, as well as with drug addiction and alcoholism. In our view, all of these conditions typically begin with, or are triggered by, emotional addictions, and it is emotional addictions that typically begin the cycles of disrupted sleep that further drive an individual into chronic states of non-homeostasis.

We also suggest that emotional addictions can profoundly disrupt the adaptive function of dreaming. It seems extremely likely that natural selection would have used the phenomenon of dreaming to serve an adaptive, functional purpose.[183] While the precise functional significance of dreaming has still not been established, psychologists such as Carl Jung have suggested that dreams serve a balancing function in the organism. For instance, if conscious thought in waking life becomes unbalanced or one-sided, dreams may alert the dreamer to neglected parts of the self, or to important knowledge or insights that the dreamer has unconscious access to, but is blocking from reaching waking consciousness.[184] Such an evolutionary adaptation could be seen as a higher-level homeostatic function, comparable to the homeostatic function of non-dreaming sleep. If any animal is to survive in the wild, all functional systems within the animal need to be geared towards achieving and maintaining homeostasis.

We suggest that the adaptive, homeostatic function of dreaming is frequently disrupted in modern life by various emotional addictions. Much as they do in waking life, emotional addictions, we suggest, influence dreams such that dream scenarios are often created or manufactured primarily to evoke negative affects in the dreamer, supplying dysfunctional payoffs driven by biochemical addiction.

"Using" dreams, in which a recovering drug addict dreams about using a drug, with many or all of the associated affects, appear to be an almost universal feature of recovery from addiction to drugs such as cocaine.[185] During the first month of one drug rehabilitation program, for example, 89% of patients reported drug-using dreams.[186] And just as actual drug relapse is often triggered by stressful events, drug-using dreams in recovering addicts appear to be also frequently triggered by specific stressors.[187] We suggest that many features of dreams in people who are not drug-abusers, but who suffer from emotional addictions, are similarly influenced by the drive for dysfunctional, non-homeostatic payoffs.

Perhaps the clearest example of such non-drug "addiction" dreams, in this sense, are the nightmares associated with post-traumatic stress disorder (PTSD), which often closely reproduce the initial trauma.[188] While, in hunter-gatherers, nightmares following traumas almost certainly have functional purposes – for example, to habituate the dreamer to the memory of a trauma – the nightmares associated with PTSD are widely viewed as being dysfunctional.[189] Van der Kolk and Greenberg[190] also suggested that the nightmares seen with PTSD can become part of the "addiction to trauma," delivering endorphin rewards to the brain. We have again extended this notion in proposing that a significant proportion of dream elements found in dreams of people living in industrialized cultures, such as the elements found in anxiety dreams, are driven by biochemical addiction.

In modern life, nightmares are very commonly experienced by children who sleep alone in an isolated room,[191] a completely unnatural circumstance that would never occur among hunter-gatherers. In hunter-gatherers, until the ages of about 3 or 4, when infants are typically weaned, infants sleep directly next to their mothers. Thereafter, children will sleep in the same huts as either their parents or other close relatives.[192] When modern children suffer from repeated nightmares, their nightmares often disappear when someone else sleeps in the same room with them.[193]

The mesolimbic dopamine circuit appears to be intimately involved in the generation of dreams,[194] and strong dopamine activation has been observed in reward areas such as the ventral tegmental area during REM sleep, the sleep phase during which dreaming mentation typically occurs.[195] The stress response also appears to be frequently activated during dreams, as cortisol levels commonly rise during the REM sleep phases.[196] Wong et al.[197] reported that patients with melancholic depression maintain elevated levels of norepinephrine and cortisol during sleep, consistent with a continued state of hyperarousal during sleep and dreaming.

A great deal of evidence suggests that continuity exists between waking life concerns and the subject matter involved in dreams. People with lower overall measures of well-being tend to experience more negative emotions and interactions during their dreams compared to individuals with higher levels of well-being, and also have more recurrent dreams, which are typically associated with negative emotions.[198] We suggest that an individual's specific addictions during waking life will frequently be perpetuated and reinforced during dreaming life. Just as it is largely the unconscious mind, based in procedural memory,[199] that engineers dysfunctional payoffs in waking life, it is the unconscious mind that creates dream scenarios that serve to deliver dysfunctional payoffs during dreaming life. This notion is similar to Freud's suggestion that dreams filled with negative emotions may represent the fulfillment of masochistic wishes.[200]

Just as depressives are well-known to have preferential access to painful thoughts during waking life, studies have also shown that the dreams of depressives very frequently contain episodes in which the dreamer is humiliated, rejected, or defeated.[201] In waking life, people with clinical depression have been shown to release endogenous opiates when asked to think of painful thoughts. If emotionally painful feelings release endogenous opiates during waking life, they may also do so during dreaming life, perpetuating the addictions to negative emotional states that we suggest lie at the heart of all depressive disorders. The observed activation of reward areas during dreaming[202] is consistent with this proposal.

Some dreams containing negative affects may well serve functional purposes, such as warning of a true danger to the emotional or physical well being of the dreamer.[203] But we suggest that when anxiety dreams, for example, are repeated and serve no discernible functional purpose, they are likely to be a manifestation of an addiction to anxiety. This is not to say that anxiety dreams are "nothing but" manifestations of addiction – the specific circumstances in the dream may also be significant, and may point to higher levels of meaning, or to traumas that the dreamer has not yet resolved. Indeed, all addictions arise from subtle or overt traumas, and the manner in which each addiction is manifested points to the nature of the trauma that needs to be healed for the addiction itself to be resolved and overcome. If we are correct that, at least in modern life, dreams frequently become hijacked by addiction, identifying the addictive elements in dreams will allow the natural homeostatic functions of dreams to become more prominent.

Play and Addiction

Play behavior probably evolved primarily to allow animals, particularly young animals, to practice and enhance, in a relatively safe manner, social and motor skills that are necessary for survival and reproduction.[204] Play behavior is generally only engaged in when other basic survival concerns have been addressed, and when the prospects for survival are generally favorable. Young vervet monkeys in East Africa, for example, will not play in dry years when food is scarce.[205] In the human lineage, the play instinct has given rise to an enormous and unique diversity of play-like behaviors and activities, such as verbal humor, art, and music.[206]

Hunter-gatherers, when not facing severe survival threats, spend a great deal of time engaging in play-like behaviors, such as story-telling, dancing, and singing, and also frequently mix play and more necessary "work" activities.[207] When basic survival needs have been met, and no threats to survival are apparent or imminent, most mammals usually either play or rest.[208] This appears to be the case with human hunter-gatherers as well, although the range of play activities is far broader than for any other animal. Play behavior, we suggest, is both a reflection of being in homeostasis, and also a homeostatic state that, in mammals in particular, delivers biochemical payoffs that are critical to the healthy, homeostatic drive.

As with dreaming, the mesolimbic dopamine system is intimately involved in play. In humans, many play behaviors, such as gambling, are clearly prone to addiction. Compulsive gambling, for example, has effects on reward circuits that are nearly identical to the effects of addictive drugs.[209] Dopamine agonists frequently increase play behavior, whereas dopamine antagonists frequently diminish play behavior.[210] Play often also involves intense affective states that presumably create significant dopamine and ß-endorphin payoffs. Singing and dancing, for example, are joyous and frequent activities that are practiced universally in hunter-gatherer cultures, acting as a cohesive social force within the band.[211] Blood and Zatorre[212] found that an antagonist to the μ opioid receptor, the receptor type to which ß-endorphin primarily binds, blocks the pleasurable feeling of "chills" that human subjects can feel when listening to music, suggesting that listening to pleasing music releases significant quantities of ß-endorphin.

We suggest that functional play behavior – the type of play expressed in our hunter-gatherer ancestors – is corrupted by biochemical addiction in several ways. First, and perhaps most important, most addictions reduce overall play-like behavior because the addiction creates the illusion of an imminent risk to survival prospects. For example, the brain interprets chronic, irrational anxiety or worry as indicating that a significant survival threat may be looming, and thus engenders the feeling that engaging in play behavior would be imprudent. Second, the play behavior itself, as with compulsive gambling, can itself become an addiction.[213] As with all other addictions, play behaviors like gambling become addictive when they lead to compulsive craving and become associated with negative emotional or physical states that become increasingly dominant as the addiction proceeds – that is, an increasing proportion of the biochemical payoffs associated with the behavior will be derived from painful, distressing, non-homeostatic states. Third, in modern life in particular, addiction frequently robs various play behaviors of the potential pleasures and joys those behaviors can uniquely provide.

By a number of accounts, for example, play in hunter-gatherers is typically not overtly competitive, and is frequently almost completely non-competitive.[214] In modern cultures, there is a remarkable obsession not only with winning games that are overtly competitive, but also "winning" at play activities, such as playing music or dancing, that are *not* intrinsically competitive. Lowen[215] viewed the western obsession with winning as reflecting a culture that fosters narcissistic personalities who often use the experience of winning and the attainment of power as overcompensations for feelings of inferiority. While the drive to win certain competitions can significantly improve status – and can therefore be considered, at least at one level, as representing a functional drive state – many modern competitions or games that confer minimal, if any, benefits to status, are frequently engaged in with an exaggerated desire to win. Such a drive is very likely to be non-homeostatic.

The purest form of play, the type of play frequently seen in hunter-gatherers, is a state of "flow," in which the participant is completely engaged in the present moment, with no thoughts about the future or the past, and without feelings of "less than." The state of flow is the state that all athletes and artists seek, but that extremely few, at least in the modern world, consistently achieve.[216] The state of flow is a purely homeostatic state. Feeling self-conscious or "judged" by other people is a reflection of subjective low status, and drives the person who feels judged out of a state of flow and into a state of non-homeostasis. Similarly, if in the midst of play a person feels unduly anxious or desirous or is thinking about the past or the future, there can be no state of flow and no pure, homeostatic play. Therefore, addiction to various non-homeostatic states can very easily corrupt the experience of play. When play is consistently corrupted, this potential source of homeostatic payoffs that is so vital to human well-being is greatly diminished in both quality and quantity, and it becomes more likely that non-homeostatic states will be dysfunctionally used to deliver biochemical payoffs. Furthermore, play, like dreaming, is a means of discovering and fulfilling an individual's "higher" homeostatic goals and aspirations, such as spiritual or artistic self-fulfillment. When addiction corrupts play, these higher aspirations frequently become blocked or stymied.

Emotional Addictions and Psychopathology

While all psychopathologies clearly have a strong genetic basis, in most cases environmental triggers also appear to be necessary for the full expression of psychopathology. Schizophrenia, for example, is a heterogeneous and complex disorder, with heritability estimates ranging from 50-85%.[217] Researchers increasingly believe that schizophrenia results from neurodevelopmental abnormalities involving any of roughly one hundred or more genes that influence basic cellular processes such as neuronal migration or cellular signaling.[218] Studies also suggest, however, that severe stress during the first trimester of pregnancy, a vital period in neurodevelopment, also significantly increases the risk of schizophrenia.[219] Other prenatal effects, such as infections with the influenza or polio virus,[220] also predispose to schizophrenia, as do physical, sexual, and emotional abuse during childhood.[221] One study, for example, found that 60% of women diagnosed with schizophrenia had experienced childhood sexual abuse.[222] Read et al.[223] suggested that well over half of all psychiatric patients, including people with major depression, schizophrenia, and borderline personality disorder, may have undergone childhood physical and sexual abuse. Hypercortisolism and other indications of a hyperreactive stress response are also one of the most consistent biological findings in people with psychiatric disorders.[224]

A large body of evidence indicates that neuroticism is a risk factor and predictor for various psychopathologies.[225] The locus G72, for instance, appears to identify at least one gene variant that creates susceptibility not only for various anxiety disorders, but also for schizophrenia, major depression, and bipolar disorder, further reinforcing the well-established familial clustering of these disorders.[226] Levels of neuroticism strongly predict the risk for major depressive disorder,[227] and it has been suggested that over half of the genetic risk for major depression is shared with the genetic risk for neuroticism.[228]

We have suggested that all neuroses are dysfunctions that arise from a biochemical addiction to various emotional states. We further suggest that neuroticism is strongly linked to other psychopathologies because emotional addictions, when combined with sensitive genetic backgrounds and histories of serious trauma, can lead to extensive damage to neurons and neural circuits arising from chronic states of stress or non-homeostasis, and that this cumulative damage can lead to the full expression of various psychopathologies. A number of studies have clearly shown that chronic stress can decrease rates of neurogenesis and result in axonal and dendritic pruning, particularly in the hippocampus and prefrontal cortex, but probably also in various other cortical regions that have been less well studied.[229] Other researchers have similarly proposed that post-traumatic stress disorder may lead to psychoses through repeated stress due to a reexperiencing of the trauma.[230]

In addition, many psychopathologies appear to be either triggered or exacerbated by disrupted sleep patterns.[231] Many factors in modern life, including the prevalence of artificial light, which has been shown to disrupt natural circadian rhythms, have contributed to a general decline in the quantity and quality of sleep.[232] It has been estimated that people now sleep about 20% less, on average, than they did even a century ago.[233] All of our brain circuits evolved in the context of hunter-gatherer life, and our hunter-gatherer ancestors probably spent a far greater amount of time sleeping that modern people generally do. Because of the apparently critical role of sleep in maintaining synaptic homeostasis in neuronal circuits,[234] such a drastic decline in sleep may contribute, for people who are genetically susceptible, to the onset and maintenance of various psychopathologies. Furthermore, disrupted sleep further drives the stress system and, particularly when combined with stress systems that are already hyperreactive from childhood traumas, may be a critical factor in the genesis of psychopathology.

Many researchers have noted that psychopathologies of all types appear to be far less frequent in traditional cultures.[235] In the ancestral environment of hunter-gatherers, childhood abuse was probably extremely rare, as were many other etiological factors that appear to contribute to psychopathology, such as emotional and social isolation, or emotional abuse.[236] We suggest that childhood traumas, because they release substantial amounts of dopamine and ß-endorphin into reward areas, and also make it far more difficult for the child to engage in states of homeostasis, often create addictions to those traumas and to the emotional states that the traumas create. Such addictions lead to chronic states of non-homeostasis and chronically overdriven stress systems that result in various types of neuronal damage, which, in sensitive genetic backgrounds, can lead to the expression of a variety of psychopathologies. Many other psychopathologies and neuroses may be, at least in part, a consequence of prenatal stress, which can similarly create a hyperreactive stress response[237] and lead to addictions to various non-homeostatic states.

In support of the notion that psychopathologies are relatively rare when human beings live in their environment of evolutionary adaptedness, strong evidence exists that hunter-gatherers are, on average, far healthier physically than people living in post-agricultural societies.[238] Although infant mortality is extremely high in hunter-gatherers compared to modern cultures, thus dragging down the average rate of mortality, a significant percentage of hunter-gatherers live into their 60s, 70s, and 80s, and many of these people are remarkably healthy.[239]

Studies suggest that many, and perhaps nearly all, chronic physical diseases or syndromes may result from modern lifestyles. For example, diabetes, acne, tooth decay, high blood pressure, and atherosclerosis are all extremely rare in hunter-gatherers, even among the elderly, and cancer rates are probably more than 100X lower than they are in industrialized cultures, even when the figures are adjusted for the relatively younger demographic profile found in hunter-gatherer populations.[240] These chronic syndromes, which are all extremely common in modern cultures, appear largely to be a consequence of unnatural diets, chronically high stress levels, and lack of sufficient physical exercise. Type 2 diabetes, for example, is extremely rare among hunter-gatherers who eat their natural diet. But if a group of hunter-gatherers begins to eat a western diet, a significant percentage will develop diabetes.[241] These individuals do not have genes "for" diabetes – they have genetic variants that make them susceptible to diabetes *only when their diets are highly unnatural*. Similarly, we suggest, relatively few hunter-gatherers ever develop serious neuroses or psychopathologies. But when the same genes that evolved in the context of hunter-gatherer life are exposed to the radically unnatural conditions of modern life, and to unnaturally overdriven stress systems, a certain percentage of people, because of their specific genetic vulnerabilities, become especially prone to developing psychiatric illnesses and neuroses.

Furthermore, we propose that all, or nearly all, psychopathologies are also *sustained* by biochemical addiction. It seems notable that psychopathologies are generally associated with symptoms that involve high levels of emotional arousal. Preferential access to painful thoughts appears to be a core feature of all types of depression, and such thoughts have been shown to release ß-endorphin in the brains of patients with major depression.[242] Such a dynamic could establish and reinforce an addictive loop that maintains the state of depression. The auditory hallucinations that are a key feature of schizophrenia very frequently involve scolding or insulting voices – probably often derived from the actual voices of abusive caregivers – who say things such as "You're no good!"[243] Such voices appear to be a more extreme manifestation of the emotionally painful and arousing thoughts and internal voices manufactured or remembered by people suffering from depression and various other neuroses. Patients with bipolar disorder swing from depressive states – which studies suggest provide substantial biochemical payoffs – to manic states associated with high levels of emotional and physical arousal, such as hyper-sexuality, that would presumably also result in substantial biochemical payoffs through activation of the stress system.

Like drug addicts, manic patients make faulty, unrealistic, impulsive decisions that often lead to painful consequences.[244]

It also seems notable that, as with drug addiction, dopamine hyper-activity is strongly associated with schizophrenia and other psychopatholo-gies.[245] Drugs that increase dopamine levels can trigger psychotic episodes that resemble those seen in paranoid schizophrenia.[246] There is also strong evidence that obsessive-compulsive disorder (OCD) similarly involves excessive dopamine neurotransmission.[247] As many researchers have noted, OCD shares other features with addiction, including obsessive thoughts, compulsive behaviors, and abnormal activation patterns in specific regions of the frontal cortex.[248]

A number of researchers have also hypothesized that schizophrenia may involve, at least in part, the dysfunctional intrusion into waking life of neuronal circuits or patterns, as yet poorly understood, that are normally operative during dreaming, creating the delusions and thought disorders that are common in both dreams and in schizophrenic states.[249] Thus the emotionally-arousing, and often cinematic, delusions seen in active schizo-phrenia may be comparable to, in our terminology, an extended addiction dream, in which dysfunctional biochemical payoffs are repeatedly delivered by the unconscious creation of emotionally arousing scenarios. Such a dynamic would be expected to provide substantial biochemical rewards, but would, in the most extreme sense, continue to drive the individual away from homeostasis, following the trajectory of all addictions.

Furthermore, schizophrenia and other psychopathologies very commonly result in severe emotional, social, and physical isolation, driving the patient further into non-homeostasis, and making it even more difficult to derive homeostatic payoffs. People with schizophrenia and borderline personality disorder (BPD), for example, typically have great difficulty establishing close, healthy relationships, and often appear to have empathy deficits.[250] Human beings are intensely social, and a large proportion of the human brain is geared towards understanding the motivations and mental states of other people, skills that are critical for healthy social interactions.[251] Studies have shown that the nucleus accumbens is strongly activated when people experience mutual cooperation with others,[252] and such interactions appear to be critical to psychological health and general homeostasis. Thus people with psychopathologies, even if their conditions are entirely genetic in origin (although this is probably rare), may be heavily biased towards deriving non-homeostatic payoffs, since homeostatic payoffs, such as those derived from healthy social interaction, are far more difficult for them to achieve. The relative unavailability of homeostatic payoffs, particularly in the unnatural circumstances of modern life, may drive people with either nascent or fully expressed psychopathologies further towards addictive, non-homeostatic payoffs derived from distressing states that may increasingly become internally generated.

We suggest that biochemical addiction is the driving force sustaining all of these psychopathologies, in which an unconscious and inexorable motivation continues to drive the patient to pursue dysfunctional behaviors that supply dysfunctional biochemical payoffs. The process is fundamentally no different from any other addiction or dysfunctional behavior. In this sense, the pathologies differ only in the specific unconscious strategies that are pursued to deliver the dysfunctional payoffs. The strategies will be strongly biased by the functional and behavioral manifestations of the pathology, which will themselves result from genetic factors, the specific nature of traumas that may have been experienced, and the specific nature of the stress-related damage to nerve cells and neuronal circuits.

Emotional Addictions, Disease, and Physical Pain

Just as an overdriven stress system appears to contribute to the development of psychopathology, a large and emerging body of evidence suggests that the development of many physical illnesses and disorders is also stress-related. Studies have shown that high stress levels are involved in the genesis of various cardiovascular diseases, and also have detrimental effects on the immune system, significantly increasing vulnerability to bacterial and viral infections, for example, and to autoimmune diseases.[253]

Because physical pain, like emotional pain, has been shown to release both dopamine and ß-endorphin into reward areas, it seems likely that various kinds of physical pain can also become addictive. Several researchers have suggested that self-mutilating human "cutters" may become addicted to the endorphin release that follows such a cut.[254] Many psychologists and psychotherapists have also long believed that emotional or psychological states can strongly influence physical states, and evidence for such effects is beginning to accumulate. Emotional states appear, at least in part, to be created by representations and meta-representations in the brain of bodily states, and Craig[255] has suggested that pathways between the brain and the body may account for the somatization of various forms of psychological distress. Psychological disorders have been found to be frequently comorbid with various types of physical pain, although the direction of causality has so far been difficult to establish.[256]

In the context of our own model, emotional states may affect physical states in at least two ways. First, the chronically elevated stress hormone levels that are typically generated by emotional addictions can result in various stress-related physical ills, such as autoimmune disorders or high blood pressure. Second, physical pain may be unconsciously created so as to generate ß-endorphin, which would both assuage and distract from emotional pain. Physical pain could also be seen as a frequent consequence and extension of the non-homeostatic, addictive drive, since the genesis of physical pain would presumably increase the overall level or proportion of biochemical payoffs that are being derived from non-homeostatic states.

It has also been clearly shown that psychological beliefs can have distinct physical effects. If people who are experiencing physical pain, for example, believe they are about to receive an opiate pain-killer, and instead receive a placebo, they will frequently autonomously release endogenous opiates within their own nervous systems that reduce their subjective levels of pain.[257] Conversely, when a placebo is given instead of an expected toxic substance, many subjects will undergo a severe stress reaction that would be an appropriate response to a truly toxic agent.[258] Other psychological states and conditions, such as those that frequently accompany various neuroses, may similarly give rise to bodily manifestations.

Addiction and the "True Self"

There is a long tradition in psychology of dividing the self into the "true self" and the "false self."[259] Carl Jung, for example, spoke of the pursuit and discovery of the true self, and the dissolution of the false self, as the ultimate goal of all psychotherapy, and the secret theme of all lasting art and literature and all major religious and spiritual traditions.[260] We suggest that the true self corresponds to the homeostatic drive, and that the persona, or false self, corresponds to the addictive drive, or the drive to non-homeostasis. In some ways, the notion of a drive to non-homeostasis is comparable to Freud's proposal of the "death instinct," which he suggested represents an innate drive towards both self-destruction and destruction of others.[261] We view the drive to non-homeostasis, however, not as an instinct, but rather as a *dysfunction* that arises from the unnatural circumstances of modern life. Freud apparently devised the notion of the death instinct primarily to explain the observed phenomena of masochism and the repetition compulsion.[262] We are proposing that both masochism and the repetition compulsion are dysfunctionally driven by biochemical addiction.

We refer to the false self as the "addiction persona," because we are proposing that a person's false self is composed entirely of that person's addictions – that is, the addiction persona, or false self, constitutes the sum total of an individual's specific addictions and addictive behaviors. Furthermore, the false self, via a semi-autonomous neural network through which various addictions become linked, can act operationally as a separate self. The separate self, or addiction persona, in our view, is merely the sum total of the neural circuits that have been hijacked by addiction, and that dysfunctionally drive a person towards non-homeostasis to deliver the dysfunctional payoffs that these states supply. The true self, we suggest, is the self without addiction. People who can rid themselves of all dysfunctional, addictive behavior will be living out of the true self, or purely out of the homeostatic drive.

Buddhism teaches that people reach an enlightened state when they rid themselves of all "attachments."[263] Our depiction and interpretation of addiction closely corresponds to the Buddhist view of attachment, and we similarly believe that the removal of all addictions leads to a psychologically or spiritually enlightened state. We have devised a therapeutic method, which we will describe elsewhere, that is based on our theoretical model and that we believe can be used to overcome any addiction, including addictions to drugs and alcohol.

The false self is an appropriate term for the addiction persona because the addiction persona is based on *lies* – lies that we tell to *ourselves*, and that only lead us further into non-homeostasis. To commit to living out of the true self is to commit to the pursuit of homeostasis, and to the homeostatic drive. While the homeostatic drive, and the state of homeostasis itself, originally evolved merely to enhance or allow the prospect of survival, in human beings the homeostatic drive can encompass other drives, such as the pursuit of spiritual, intellectual, or artistic fulfillment, that may become largely independent of simple survival or reproductive concerns. We believe that the knowledge of how addiction and the non-homeostatic drive operate can greatly enhance the pursuit of these higher goals.

Notes

1. Craig, 2003; Paulus, 2007
2. Koob, 2008; Piazza, 1997
3. Kelley & Berridge, 2002; Lekners & Tracey, 2008
4. Robinson & Berridge, 2003
5. Kelley & Berridge, 2002; Hyman & Malenka, 2001; Carelli, & Wightman, 2004; Roitman, Stuber, Phillips, Wightman, & Carelli, 2004; Wise, 2002
6. De Quervain et al., 2004
7. Wise, 2002
8. Adcock, Thangavel, Whitfield-Gabrieli, Knutson, & Gabrieli, 2006
9. Kaver & Malenka, 2007; Liu, Pu, & Poo, 2005; Ungless et al., 2003
10. Robinson & Berridge, 2003
11. Cannon & Palmiter, 2003; Fields, 2004
12. Helmuth, 2001; Hyman & Malenka, 2001; Robinson & Berridge, 2003
13. Holstege et al., 2003
14. Small, Zatorre, Dagher, Evans, & Jones-Gotman, 2001
15. Aharon et al., 2001
16. Mobbs, Greicius, Abdel-Azim, Menon & Reiss, 2003
17. Breiter, Aharon, Kahneman, Dale, & Shizgal, 2001
18. Blood & Zatorre, 2001
19. Gear, Aley, & Levine, 1999; Jensen et al., 2003; Lekners & Tracey, 2008
20. Marinelli, Quirion, & Gianoulakis, 2004
21. Marinelli et al., 2004
22. Zubieta et al., 2001
23. Sandman, Hetrick, Taylor, & Chicz-DeMet, 1997
24. Kennedy, Koeppe, Young, & Zubieta, 2006
25. Luecken & Appelhans, 2006; Pruessner, Champagne, Meaney, & Dagher, 2004
26. Becerra, Breiter, Wise, Gonzalez, & Borsook, 2001; Schmidt et al., 2002
27. Kandel, Schwartz, & Jessell, 1991, pp. 397-398
28. Cabib, & Puglisi-Allegra, 1996
29. Hnasko, Sotak, & Palmiter, 2005
30. Horvitz, 2002
31. Susskind et al., 2008
32. Darwin, 1872; De Gelder, 2006
33. Charmandari, Tsigos, & Chrousos, 2005
34. Joëls, 2006; De Kloet, 2005
35. Sabban & Kvetnansky, 2001; Sapolsky, 2004
36. Charmandari et al., 2005
37. Schmidt et al., 2002
38. Charmandari et al., 2005
39. Eisenberger & Lieberman, 2004
40. Nelson & Panksepp, 1998
41. Wand et al., 2007; Yavich & Tiihonen, 2000
42. Saal, Dong, Bonci, & Malenka, 2003
43. Koob, 2008
44. Newport & Nemeroff, 2000
45. Heim et al., 2000
46. Castillo, 1994; Gross, & Hen, 2004; Janssen et al., 2004; Read, 1998; Van der Kolk, 2003

47. Maestripieri, 2005
48. Kosten, Zhang, & Kehoe, 2003
49. Thornberg & Lyvers, 2006b; Koob, 2008
50. Jacobsen, Southwick, & Kosten, 2001; Robbins & Everitt, 1999
51. Piazza, 1997
52. Kippin, 2008
53. Sarkar, Bergman, Fisk, O'Connor, & Glover, 2007
54. Malanga, Pejchal, & Kosofsky, 2007
55. Czoty, Morgan, Shannon, Gage, & Nader, 2004
56. Morgan et al., 2002
57. Volkow & Li, 2004
58. Devries, Glasper, & Detillion, 2003
59. Dackis & O'Brien, 2005
60. Nader et al., 2006
61. Uhl, 2007
62. Morgan et al., 2002
63. Wang et al., 2001
64. Volkow & Wise, 2005
65. Keel, Klump, Miller, McGue, & Iacono, 2005; Read, 1998; Van der Kolk, 2001
66. Hnasko et al., 2005
67. Wang et al., 2001
68. Dum & Herz, 1984
69. Barbano & Cador, 2006; Wang et al., 2001
70. Berman et al., 2003
71. Eisenberger & Lieberman, 2004
72. Freud, 1920
73. Adler, 1956 , p. 271
74. Robinson & Berridge, 2003
75. Sapolsky, 2004; Charmandari et al., 2005
76. Hart, Ward, Haney, Foltin, & Fischman, 2001
77. Beck, 2006
78. Kennedy et al., 2006
79. Ressler & Mayberg, 2007
80. Luecken & Appelhans, 2006; Pruessner et al., 2004
81. Nestler & Carlezon, 2005; Sapolsky, 2004
82. Brunton and Russell, 2008
83. Pittenger & Duman, 2008
84. Segi-Nishida, Warner-Schmidt, & Duman, 2008
85. Korte, Koolhaas, Wingfield, & McEwen, 2005; Pittenger & Duman, 2008; Sapolsky, 2004
86. Nesse, 2000
87. Selye, 1976
88. Kim & Diamond, 2002
89. Dawkins, 1976
90. Maynard-Smith, 1993; Wright, 1994
91. Nesse, 2000
92. Dum & Herz, 1984
93. Robinson & Berridge, 2003
94. Schwartz & Seeley, 1997
95. Dallman et al. 2003

96. Read, 1998
97. Keel, Klump, Miller, McGue, & Iacono, 2005
98. Bowlby, 1982; Freud, 1989
99. Bugental, Martorell, & Barraza, 2003; Almert, Gunnar, Lamb, & Barthel, 2004; Sroufe, 2005
100. Belsky, 2006; O'Connor & Croft, 2001
101. Hrdy, 1999
102. Bowlby, 1982, p.xxix
103. Azar, Paquette, Zoccolillo, Baltzer, & Tremblay, 2007
104. Zonnevylle-Bender et al., 2005
105. Kinniburgh, Blaustein, & Spinazzola, 2005; Van der Kolk, 2003
106. Zhang, Parent, Weaver, & Meaney, 2004
107. Brake, Zhang, Diorio, Meaney, & Gratton, 2004
108. Bradshaw, Schore, Brown, Poole, & Moss, 2005; Fleming, O'Day, & Kraemer, 1999
109. Luecken & Appelhans, 2006; Pruessner et al., 2004
110. Belsky, 2006; Zhang et al., 2004
111. Belsky, 2006; Zhang et al., 2004
112. Belsky, 2006; Luecken & Lemery, 2004; Neborsky, 2006
113. Weaver, Meaney, & Szyf, 2006
114. Tsankova, Renthal, Kumar, & Nestler, 2007
115. Caspi et al., 2002
116. Collinshaw et al., 2007
117. Sapolsky, 2004
118. Morgan et al., 2002
119. Decker, 2000; Marmot, 2004; Steptoe et al., 2002
120. Essex, Klein, Cho, & Kalin, 2002
121. Marmot, 2004
122. Marmot, 2004, p. 89
123. Donnellan, Trzesniewski, Robins, Moffitt, & Caspi, 2005
124. Anda et al., 2002; Luecken & Lemery, 2004
125. Freud, 1989; Adler, 1956; Horney, 1950
126. Anda et al., 2002
127. Thornberg & Lyvers, 2006
128. Wright, 1994
129. Bersaglieri et al., 2004
130. Ingold, 1999
131. Konner, 2005
132. Ingold, 1999
133. Sroufe, 2005
134. Cacioppo, Hawkley, & Berntson, 2003
135. Czoty et al., 2004; Kosten, Zhang, & Kehoe, 2003
136. Eaton, Shostak, & Konner, 1988; Bird-David, 2005
137. Ingold, 1999
138. Gould, 1969; Ingold, 1999; Turnbull, 1965
139. Hill & Hurtado, 1996; Shostak, 1981; Wright, 1994
140. Smith, 2004
141. Shostak, 1981; Turnbull, 1965
142. Endicott, 1999

143. Boehm, 1999; Lenski, 1984; the Kwakiutl and other neighboring cultures on the Northwest Coast of America were exceptions to this general rule in that the unusually rich resources in the area allowed them to be sedentary hunter-gatherers. Their sedentary life and resource-rich environment led to notable social stratification.
144. Lenski, 1984
145. Glantz & Pearce, 1989
146. Fehr, Bernhard, and Rockenbach, 2008
147. Dawes, Fowler, Johnson, McElreath, & Smirnov, 2007
148. Dawkins, 1976; Wright, 1994
149. Zink et al., 2008
150. Horney, 1950
151. Hewlett & Lamb, 2005; Konner, 2005
152. Bird-David, 2005
153. Fouts et al., 2005
154. Fouts et al., 2005
155. Sears & Sears, 2001
156. Eaton et al., 1988; Hewlett, Lamb, Leyendecker, & Scholmerich, 2000
157. Evans, 2004; Sears & Sears, 2001
158. Glantz and Pearce, 1989
159. Konner, 2005; Sears & Sears, 2001
160. Eaton et al., 1988
161. Zhang et al., 2004
162. Hrdy, 1999
163. Freud, 1920
164. Van der Kolk & Greenberg, 1987
165. Pitman, van der Kolk, Orr, & Greenberg, 1990
166. Singer et al., 2006
167. De Quervain et al., 2004
168. Call & Tomasello, 2008; Raby, Alexis, Dickinson, & Clayton, 2007
169. Damasio, 1994
170. Suddendorf & Corballis, 1997
171. Kennedy et al., 2006
172. Call & Tomasello, 2008
173. Wright, 1994
174. Liebenberg, 2006
175. Horney, 1950; Jung, 1959
176. Jung, 1959
177. Melville, 1851
178. Allada, & Siegel, 2008
179. Allada & Siegel, 2008
180. Vyazovskiy, Cirelli, Pfister-Genskow, Faraguna, & Tononi, 2008
181. Plante & Winkelman, 2008
182. Benca, Obermeyer, Thisted, & Gillin, 1992
183. Bulkeley, 1994; Revonsuo, 2000
184. Bulkeley, 1994; Jung, 1974
185. Flowers, 1998
186. Reid, 2001
187. Flowers, 1998
188. McNally, 2006; van der Kolk, 1987
189. Nielsen & Germain, 2000

190. Van der Kolk and Greenberg, 1987
191. Siegel & Bulkeley, 1998
192. Hewlett & Lamb, 2005
193. Lansky, 1992, p. 344
194. Solms, 2000
195. Dahan et al., 2007
196. Shafton, 1995
197. Wong et al., 2000
198. Pesant & Zadra, 2006; Zadra, Desjardins, & Marcotte, 2006
199. Kalivas & O'Brien, 2008
200. Bulkeley, 1997; Freud, 1920
201. Beck, 2006; Shafton, 1995
202. Dahan et al., 2007
203. Revonsuo, 2000
204. Burghardt, 2005
205. Bateson, 2005
206. Huizinga, 1950
207. Shostak, 1981; Turnbull, 1965
208. Burghardt, 2005
209. Holden, 2001
210. Siviy, 1998
211. Barac, 1999; Williams, 1980
212. Blood and Zatorre, 2001
213. Holden, 2001; Reuter, 2005
214. Kamei, 2005; Eaton, 1988, pp. 226-227; Shostak, 1981, pp. 108-109
215. Lowen,1985
216. Gardner, 2003
217. Kandel, Schwartz, & Jessell, 2000; Mitchell, Elliott, & Woodruff, 2001
218. Walsh et al., 2008; Yeo, Gangestad, Edgar, & Thoma, 1999
219. Khashan et al., 2008
220. Dalman et al., 2008
221. Braehler et al., 2004; Holowka, King, Saheb, Pukall, & Brunet, 2003
222. Castillo, 2003
223. Read et al., 1998
224. Oswald, 2006
225. Khan, Jacobson, Gardner, Prescott, & Kendler, 2005
226. Rietschel et al., 2008
227. Kendler, Gatz, Gardner, & Pedersen, 2006
228. Levinson, 2006
229. Korte et al., 2005; Pittenger & Duman, 2008
230. Kilcommons & Morrison, 2005
231. Plante & Winkelman, 2008
232. Moore-Ede, 1993
233. Ferrara & De Gennaro, 2001
234. Vyazovskiy et al., 2008
235. Allen, 1997
236. Holowka et al., 2003
237. Kaiser, & Sachser, 2005
238. Cohen, 1989
239. Holden, 2006; Hrdy, 1999

240. Eaton et al., 1988; Eaton & Eaton, 1999
241. Cohen, 1989; Eaton & Eaton, 1999
242. Kennedy et al., 2006
243. Johns & McGuire,1999
244. Harvey, 2008
245. Arnsten, 1997
246. Kapur, Mizrahi, & Li, 2005
247. Hesse et al., 2005
248. Kringelbach, 2005; Volkow & Fowler, 2000
249. Hobson, 1994; Jung, 1974
250. Decety & Hodges, 2006
251. Blakemore, 2008
252. Rilling et al., 2002
253. Sapolsky, 2004
254. Strong, 1998; Van der Kolk & Greenberg, 1987
255. Craig, 2002
256. Scott et al., 2007
257. Benedetti, Mayberg, Wager, Stohler, & Zubieta, 2005
258. Johansen, Brox, & Flaten, 2003
259. Jung, 1971; Laing, 1969; Winnicott, 1986
260. Jung, 1966
261. Freud, 1920
262. Freud, 1920
263. Suzuki, 1960

References

Adcock, R. A., Thangavel, A., Whitfield-Gabrieli, S., Knutson, B., & Gabrieli, J. D. E. (2006). Reward-motivated learning: Mesolimbic activation precedes memory formation. *Neuron, 50*, 507-517.

Adler, A. (Ansbacher, H. L. & Ansbacher, R. R. Eds). (1956). *The individual psychology of Alfred Adler.* New York: HarperPerennial.

Aharon, I., Etcoff, N., Ariely, D., Chabris, C. F., O'Connor, E., & Breiter, H. C. (2001). Beautiful Faces have Variable Reward Value: fMRI and behavioral evidence. *Neuron, 32*, 537-551.

Aharon, I., Becerraa, L., Chabris, C F., & Borsooka, D. (2006). Noxious heat induces fMRI activation in two anatomically distinct clusters within the nucleus accumbens. *Neuroscience Letters, 392*, 159-164.

Allada, R., & Siegel, J. M. (2008). Unearthing the phylogenetic roots of sleep. *Current Biology, 18*, R670-R679.

Allen, J. S. (1997). At issue: Are traditional societies schizophrenogenic? *Schizophrenia Bulletin, 23* (3), 357-364.

Almert, L., Gunnar, M. R., Lamb, M. E., & Barthel, M. (2004). Transition to Child Care: Associations with infant-mother attachment, infant negative emotion, and cortisol elevations. *Child Development, 75* (3), 639-650.

Anda, R. F., Whitfield, C. L., Felitti, V. J., Chapman, D., Edwards, V. J., Dube, S. R., & Williamson, D. F. (2002). Adverse childhood experiences, alcoholic parents, and later risk of alcoholism and depression. *Psychiatric Services, 53* (8), 1001-1009.

Arnsten, A. F. T. (1997). Catecholamine regulation of the prefrontal cortex. *Journal of Psychopharmacology, 11* (2), 151-162.

Azar, R., Paquette, D., Zoccolillo, M., Baltzer, F. & Tremblay, R. E. (2007). The association of major depression, conduct disorder, and maternal overcontrol with a failure to show a cortisol buffered response in 4-month-old infants of teenage mothers. *Biol Psychiatry, 62*, 573-579.

Barac, V. (1999). From primitive to pop: foraging and post-foraging hunter-gatherer music. In Lee, R. B., & Daly, R. (Eds.), *The Cambridge encyclopedia of hunters and gatherers.* Cambridge, UK: Cambridge University Press.

Barbano, M. F., & Cador, M. (2006). Differential regulation of the consummatory, motivational and anticipatory aspects of feeding behavior by dopaminergic and opioidergic drugs. *Neuropsychopharmacology. 31*, 1371-1381.

Bateson, P. (2005). The role of play in the evolution of great apes and humans. In Pellegrini, A. D., & Smith, P. K. (Eds.) *The nature of play: Great apes and humans.* New York: The Guilford Press.

Becerra, L, Breiter, H. C., Wise, R., Gonzalez, R. G., & Borsook, D. (2001). Reward circuitry activation by noxious thermal stimuli. *Neuron, 32*, 927-946.

Beck, A. T. (2006). How an anomalous finding led to a new system of psychotherapy. *Nature Medicine, 12* (10), 1139-1141.

Belsky, J. (2006). Determinants and consequences of infant-parent attachment. In Balter, L. & Tamis-LeMonda, C. (Eds.), *Child Psychology: A Handbook of Contemporary Issues*. New York: Psychology Press.

Benca, R. M., Obermeyer, W. H., Thisted, R. A., & Gillin, J. C. (1992). Sleep and psychiatric disorders. A meta-analysis. *Archives of General Psychiatry 49(8)*, 651.

Benedetti, F., Mayberg, H. S., Wager, T. D., Stohler, C. S., & Zubieta, J. (2005). Neurobiological mechanisms of the placebo effect. *J. Neurosci., 25* (45), 10390-10402.

Berman, S. M., Ozkaragoz, T., Noble, E. P., Antolin, T., Sheen, C., Siddarth, P., et al. (2003). Differential associations of sex and D2 dopamine receptor (DRD2) genotype with negative affect and other substance abuse risk markers in children of alcoholics. *Alcohol, 30*, 201-210.

Bersaglieri, T., Sabeti, P. C., Patterson, N., Vanderploeg, T., Schaffner, S. F., Drake, J. A., et al. (2004). Genetic signatures of strong recent positive selection at the lactase gene. *Am. J. Hum. Genet., 74*, 1111-1120.

Bird-David, N. (2005). Studying children in "Hunter-Gatherer" societies. In Hewlett, B. S., & Lamb, M. E (Eds.), *Hunter-gatherer childhoods*. New Jersey: Transaction Publishers.

Blakemore, S-J. (2008). The social brain in adolescence. *Nature Reviews Neuroscience, 9,* 267-277.

Blood, A. J., & Zatorre, R. J. (2001). Intensely pleasurable responses to music correlate with activity in brain regions implicated in reward and emotion. *PNAS, 98* (20), 11818-11823.

Boehm, C. (1999). *Hierarchy in the forest: The evolution of egalitarian behavior*. Cambridge, MA : Harvard University Press.

Bowlby, J. 1(982). *Attachment*. New York: Basic.

Bradshaw, G. A., Schore, A. N., Brown, J. L., Poole, J. H., & Moss, C. J. (2005). Social trauma: Early disruption of attachment can affect the physiology, behaviour and culture of animals and humans over generations. *Nature, 433*, 807.

Braehler, C., Holowka, D., Brunet, A., Beaulieu, S., Baptista, T., Debruille, J-B, et al. (2004). Diurnal cortisol in schizophrenia patients with childhood trauma. *Schizophrenia Research, 79*, 353-354.

Brake, W. G., Zhang, T. Y., Diorio, J., Meaney, M. J., & Gratton, A. (2004). Influence of early postnatal rearing conditions on mesocorticolimbic dopamine and behavioural responses to psychostimulants and stressors in adult rats. *European Journal of Neuroscience, 19*, 1863-1874.

Breiter, H. C., Aharon, I., Kahneman, D., Dale, A., & Shizgal, P. (2001). Functional imaging of neural responses to expectancy and experience of monetary gains and losses. *Neuroimage, 21*, 1155-1166.

Brunton, P. J., & Russell, J. A. (2008). The expectant brain: Adapting for motherhood. *Nature Reviews Neuroscience, 9*, 11-25.

Bugental, D. B., Martorell, G. A., & Barraza, V. (2003). The hormonal costs of subtle forms of infant maltreatment. *Hormones and Behavior, 43*, 237-244.

Bulkeley, K. (1994). *The wilderness of dreams.* Albany, NY: State University of New York Press.

Burghardt, G. M. (2005). *The genesis of animal play.* Cambridge, MA: The MIT Press.

Cabib, S., & Puglisi-Allegra, S. (1996). Stress, depression and the mesolimbic dopamine system. *Psychopharmacology, 128*, 331-342.

Cacioppo, J. T., Hawkley, L. C., & Berntson, G. G. (2003). The anatomy of loneliness. *Current Directions in Psychological Science, 12* (3), 71-74.

Call, J. & Tomasello, M. (2008). Does the chimpanzee have a theory of mind? 30 years later. *Trends in Cognitive Sciences, 12* (5), 187-192.

Cannon, C. M & Palmiter, R. D. (2003). Reward without dopamine. *J. Neurosci., 23* (34), 10827-10831.

Carelli, R. M., & Wightman, R. M. (2004). Functional microcircuitry in the accumbens underlying drug addiction: Insights from real-time signaling during behavior. *Current Opinion in Neurobiology, 14*, 763-768.

Caspi, A., McClay, J., Moffitt, T. E., Mill, J., Martin, J., Craig, I. W., Taylor, Al, & Poulton, R. (2002). Role of genotype in the cycle of violence in maltreated children. *Science, 297*, 851-854.

Castillo, R. J. (1994). Spirit possession in South Asia, dissociation or hysteria? *Culture, Medicine, and Psychiatry, 18*, 1-21.

Castillo, R. J. (2003). Trance, functional psychosis, and culture. *Psychiatry, 66* (1), 9-21.

Charmandari, E., Tsigos, C., & Chrousos, G. (2005). Endocrinology of the stress response. *Annu. Rev. Physiol., 67*, 259-284.

Cohen, M. N. (1989). *Health & the rise of civilization.* New Haven: Yale University Press.

Collinshaw, S., Pickles, A., Messer, J., Rutter, M., Shearer, C., & Maughan, B. (2007). Resilience to adult psychopathology following childhood maltreatment: Evidence from a community sample. *Child Abuse & Neglect, 31*, 211-229.

Craig, A. D. (2003). A new view of pain as a homeostatic emotion. *Trends in Neuroscience, 26* (6), 303-307.

Czoty, P. W., Morgan, D., Shannon, E. E., Gage, H. D., & Nader, M. A. (2004). Characterization of dopamine D_1 and D_2 receptor function in socially housed cynomolgus monkeys self-administering cocaine. *Psychopharmacology, 174*, 381-388.

Dackis, C., & O'Brien, C. (2005). Neurobiology of addiction: Treatment and public policy ramifications. *Nature, 8* (11), 1431-1436.

Dahan, L., Astier, B., Vautrelle, N., Urbain, N., Kocsis, B., & Chouvet, G. (2007). Prominent burst firing of dopaminergic neurons in the ventral tegmental area during paradoxical sleep. *Neuropsychopharmacology, 32*, 1232-1241.

Dallman, M. F., Pecoraro, N., Akana, S. F., la Fleur, S. E., Gomez, F., Houshyar, H., et al. (2003). Chronic stress and obesity: A new view of "comfort food". *PNAS, 100* (20), 11696-11701.

Dalman, C., Allebeck, P., Gunnell, D., Harrison, G., Kristensson, K., Lewis, G. et al. (2008). Infections in the CNS during childhood and the risk of subsequent psychotic illness: A cohort study of more than one million Swedish subjects. *Am J Psychiatry, 165* (1), 59-65.

Damasio, A. R. (1994). *Descartes' error.* New York: Avon Books.

Darwin, C. (1872). *The expression of the emotions in man and animals.* Oxford: Oxford University Press.

Dawes, C. T., Fowler, J. H., Johnson, T., McElreath, R., & Smirnov, O. (2007). Egalitarian motives in humans. *Nature, 446*, 794-796.

Dawkins, R. (1976). *The selfish gene.* Oxford: Oxford University Press.

Decety, J., Hodges, S. D. (2006). The social neuroscience of empathy. *In: Bridging social psychology: Benefits of transdisciplinary approaches (Van Lange, P. A. M., ed.)*, 103-109. Mahwah: Erlbaum.

Decker, S. A. (2000). Salivary cortisol and social status among Dominican men. *Hormones and Behavior, 38*, 29-38.

De Gelder, B. (2006). Towards the neurobiology of emotional body language. *Nature Reviews Neuroscience, 7*, 242-249.

De Kloet, E. R. , Joels, M., & Holsboer, F. (2005). Stress and the Brain: From adaptation to disease. *Nature Reviews Neuroscience, 6*, 463-475.

De Quervain, D. J. F., Fischbacher, U., Treyer, V., Schellhammer, M., Schnyder, U., Buck, A., & Fehr, E. (2004). The neural basis of altruistic punishment. *Science, 305*, 1254-1258.

DeVries, A. C., Glasper, E. R., & Detillion, C. E. (2003). Social modulation of stress responses. *Physiology & Behavior, 79*, 399-407.

Donnellan, M B., Trzesniewski, K. H., Robins, R. W., Moffitt, T. E., & Caspi, A. (2005). Low self-esteem is related to aggression, antisocial behavior, and delinquency. *Psychological Science, 305*, 328-335.

Dum, J., & Herz, A. (1984). Endorphinergic modulation of neural reward systems indicated by behavioral changes. *Pharmacol Biochem Behav, 21* (2), 259-266.

Eaton, S. B., Shostak, M., & Konner, M. (1988). *The Paleolithic prescription.* New York: Harper & Row.

Eaton, S. B., & Eaton, S. B. III. (1999). Hunter-gatherers and human health. In Lee, R. B., & Daly, R. (Eds.), *The Cambridge encyclopedia of hunters and gatherers.* Cambridge, UK: Cambridge University Press.

Eisenberger, N. I., & Lieberman, M D. (2004). Why rejection hurts: a common neural alarm system for physical and social pain. *Trends in Cognitive Science, 8* (7), 294-300.

Endicott, K. L. (1999). Gender relations in hunter-gatherer societies. In Lee, R. B., & Daly, R. (Eds.), *The Cambridge encyclopedia of hunters and gatherers.* Cambridge, UK: Cambridge University Press.

Essex, M. J., Klein, M. H., Cho, E., & Kalin, N. H. (2002). Maternal stress beginning in infancy may sensitize children to later stress exposure: Effects on cortisol and behavior. *Biol Psychiatry, 52*, 776-784.

Evans, R. (2004). *Family Matters: How schools can cope with the crisis in childrearing.* San Francisco: Jossey-Bass.

Fehr, E., Bernhard, H., & Rockenbach, B. (2008). Egalitarianism in young children. *Nature, 454*, 1079-1084.

Ferrara, M., & De Gennaro, L. (2001). How much sleep do we need? *Sleep Med Rev, 5* (2), 155-179.

Fields, H. (2004). State-dependent opioid control of pain. *Nature Reviews Neuroscience, 5*, 565-575.

Fleming, A. S., O'Day, D. H, & Kraemer, G. W. (1999). Neurobiology of mother-infant interactions: experience and central nervous system plasticity cross development and generations. *Neuroscience and Biobehavioral Reviews, 23*, 673-685.

Flowers, L. K., & Zweben, J. E. (1998). The changing role of "using" dreams in addiction recovery. *Journal of Substance Abuse Treatment 15* (3), 193-200.

Fouts, H. N., Hewlett, B. S., & Lamb, M. E. (2005). Parent-offspring weaning conflicts among the Bofi farmers and foragers of central Africa. *Current Anthropology, 46* (1), 29-50.

Freud, S. (1920). *Beyond the pleasure principle.* New York: Barnes & Noble.

Freud, S. (1952). *On Dreams.* New York: Norton.

Freud, S. (Gay, P. Ed.). (1989). *The Freud reader*. New York: Norton.

Gardner, H. (1993). *Creating minds*. New York: Basic.

Gear, R. W., Aley, K. O., & Levine, J. D. (1999). Pain-induced analgesia mediated by mesolimbic reward circuits. *J. Neurosci. 19* (16), 7175-7181.

Glantz, K. & Pearce, J. K. (1989). *Exiles from Eden: Psychotherapy from an evolutionary perspective*. New York: W. W. Norton.

Gould, R. A. (1969). *Yiwara: Foragers of the Australian desert*. New York: Scribner.

Gross, C., & Hen, R. (2004). The developmental origins of anxiety. *Nature Reviews Neuroscience, 5*, 545-552.

Hart, C. L., Ward, A. S., Haney, M., Foltin, R. W., & Fischman, M. W. (2001). Methamphetamine self-administration by humans. *Psychopharmacology, 157*, 75-81.

Harvey, A. G. (2008). Sleep and circadian rhythms in bipolar disorder: Seeking synchrony, harmony, and regulation. *Am J Psychiatry, 165* (7), 820-829.

Heim, C., Newport, D. J., Heit, S., Graham, Y. P., Wilcox, M., Bonsall, R., Miller, A. H., & Nemeroff, C. B. (2000). Pituitary-adrenal and autonomic responses to stress in women after sexual and physical abuse in childhood. *JAMA, 284* (5), 592-597.

Helmuth, L. (2001). Beyond the pleasure principle. *Science, 294*, 983-984.

Hesse, S., Müller, U., Lincke, T., Barthel, H., Villmann, T., Angermeyer, M. C., et al. (2005). Serotonin and dopamine transporter imaging in patients with obsessive-compulsive disorder. *Psychiatry Research: Neuroimaging, 140*, 63-72.

Hewlett, B. S., Lamb, M. E., Leyendecker, B., & Scholmerich, A. (2000). Internal working models, trust, and sharing among foragers. *Current Anthropology, 41* (2), 287-297.

Hewlett, B. S., & Lamb, M. E. (2005). Emerging issues in the study of hunter-gatherer children. In Hewlett, B. S., & Lamb, M. E (Eds.), *Hunter-gatherer childhoods*. New Jersey: Transaction Publishers.

Hill, K., & Hurtado, A. M. (1996). *Ache life history*. New York: Aldine De Gruyter.

Hnasko, T. S., Sotak, B. N., & Palmiter, R. D. (2005). Morphine reward in dopamine-deficient mice. *Nature, 438*, 854-857.

Hobson, J. A. (1994). *The chemistry of conscious states*. New York: Little, Brown and Company.

Holden, C. (2001). 'Behavioral' addictions: Do they exist? *Science, 294*, 980-982.

Holden, C. (2006). Long-ago peoples may have been long in the tooth. *Science, 312*, 1867.

Holowka, D. W., King, S., Saheb, D., Pukall, M., & Brunet, A. (2003). Childhood abuse and dissociative symptoms in adult schizophrenia. *Schizophrenia Research, 60*, 87-90.

Holstege, G., Georgiadis, J. R., Paans, A. M., Meiners, L. C., van der Graaf, F. H., & Reinders, A. A. (2003). Brain activation during human male ejaculation. *J. Neurosci., 23* (27), 9185-9193.

Horney, K. (1950/1991). *Neurosis and human growth.* New York: Norton.

Horvitz, J. C. (2002). Dopamine gating of glutamatergic sensorimotor and incentive motivational input signals to the striatum. *Behavioural Brain Research, 137*, 65-74.

Hrdy, S. B. (1999). *Mother nature: Maternal instincts and how they shape the human species.* New York: Ballantine Books.

Huizinga, J. (1950). *Homo ludens: A study of the play element in culture.* Boston: The Beacon Press.

Hyman, S. E., & Malenka, R. C. (2001). Addiction and the Brain: Neurobiology of compulsion and its persistence. *Nature Reviews Neuroscience, 2*, 695-703.

Ingold, T. (1999). On the social relations of the hunter-gatherer band. In Lee, R. B., & Daly, R. (Eds.), *The Cambridge encyclopedia of hunters and gatherers.* Cambridge, UK: Cambridge University Press.

Jacobsen, L. K., Southwick, S. M., & Kosten, T. R. (2001). Substance use disorders in patients with posttraumatic stress disorder: a review of the literature. *Am J Psychiatry, 158* (8), 1184-1190.

Janssen, I., Krabbendam, L., Bak, M., Hanssen, M., Vollebergh, W., De Graaf, R., & Van Os, J. (2004). Childhood abuse as a risk factor for psychotic experiences. *Acta Psychiatr Scand, 109*, 38-45.

Jensen, J., McIntosh, A. R., Crawley, A. P., Mikulis, D. J., Remington, G., & Kapur, S. (2003). Direct activation of the ventral striatum in anticipation of aversive stimuli. *Neuron, 40*, 1251-1257.

Joëls, M., Pu, Z., Wiegert, O., Oitzl, M. S., & Krugers, H. J. (2006). Learning under stress: how does it work?. *Trends in Cognitive Science, 10* (4), 152-158.

Johansen, O., Brox, J., & Flaten, M. A. (2003). Placebo and nocebo responses, cortisol, and circulating beta-endorphin. *Psychosomatic Medicine, 65*, 786-790.

Johns, L. C., & McGuire, P. K. (1999). Verbal self-monitoring and auditory hallucinations in schizophrenia. *The Lancet, 353*, 469-470.

Jung, C. G. (1959). *Aion.* Princeton, NJ: Princeton University Press.

Jung, C. G. (1966). *The spirit in man, art, and literature.* Princeton, NJ: Princeton University Press.

Jung, C. G. (1971). *Psychological types.* Princeton, NJ: Princeton University Press.

Jung, C. G. (1974). *Dreams*. Princeton, NJ: Princeton University Press.

Kaiser, S., & Sachser, N. (2005). The effects of prenatal social stress on behaviour: mechanisms and function. *Neuroscience and Biobehavioral Reviews, 29*, 283-294.

Kalivas, P. W., & O'Brien, C. (2008). Drug addiction as a pathology of staged neuroplasticity. *Neuropsychopharmacololgy Reviews, 33*, 166-180.

Kamei, N. (2005). Play among Baka children in Cameroon. In Hewlett, B. S., & Lamb, M. E (Eds.), *Hunter-gatherer childhoods*. New Jersey: Transaction Publishers.

Kandel, E. R., Schwartz, J. H., & Jessell, T. M. (Eds.) (1991). Principles of neural science, Third Edition. New York: Elsevier.

Kandel, E. R., Schwartz, J. H., & Jessell, T. M. (Eds.) (2000). Principles of neural science, Fourth Edition. New York: McGraw-Hill.

Kapur, S., Mizrahi, R., & Li, M. (2005). From dopamine to salience to psychosis – linking biology, pharmacology and phenomenology of psychosis. *Schizophrenia Research, 79*, 59-68.

Kauer, J. A., & Malenka, R. C. (2007). Synaptic plasticity and addiction. *Nature Reviews Neuroscience, 8*, 844- 858.

Keel, P. K., Klump, K. L., Miller, K. B., McGue, M., & Iacono, W. G. (2005). Shared transmission of eating disorders and anxiety disorders. *Int J Eat Disord, 38* (2), 99-105.

Kelley, A. E., & Berridge, K. C. (2002). The neuroscience of natural rewards: Relevance to addictive drugs. *The Journal of Neuroscience, 22* (9), 3306-3311.

Kendler, K. S., Gatz, M., Gardner, C. O., & Pedersen, N. L. (2006). Personality and major depression. *Arch Gen Psychiatry, 63*, 109-114.

Kennedy, S. E., Koeppe, R. A., Young, E. A., & Zubieta, J-K. (2006). Dysregulation of endogenous opioid emotion regulation circuitry in major depression in women. *Arch Gen Psychiatry, 63*, 1199-1208.

Khan, A. A., Jacobson, K. C., Gardner, C. O., Prescott, C. A., & Kendler, K. S. (2005). Personality and comorbidity of common psychiatric disorders. *The Brtitsh Journal of Psychiatry, 186*, 190-196.

Khashan, A. S., Abel, K. M., McNamee, R., Pedersen, M. G., Webb, R. T., Baker, P. N., et al. (2008). Higher risk of offspring schizophrenia following antenatal maternal exposure to severe adverse life events. *Archives of General Psychiatry 65* (2), 146-152.

Kilcommons, A. M., & Morrison, A. P. (2005). Relationships between trauma and psychosis: an exploration of cognitive and dissociative factors. *Acta Psychiatr Scand, 112*, 351-359.

Kim, J. J., & Diamond, D. M. (2002). The stressed hippocampus, synaptic plasticity and lost memories. *Nature Reviews Neuroscience, 3*, 453-462.

Kinniburgh, K. J., Blaustein, M., & Spinazzola, J. (2005). Attachment, self-regulation, and competency. *Psychiatric Annals, 35* (5), 424-430.

Kippin, T. E., Szumlinski, K. K., Kapasova, Z., Rezner, B., & See, R. E. (2008). Prenatal stress enhances responsiveness to cocaine. *Neuropsychopharmacology, 33*, 769-782.

Konner, M. (2005). Hunter-gatherer infancy and childhood: The !Kung and others. In Hewlett, B. S., & Lamb, M. E (Eds.), *Hunter-gatherer childhoods.* New Jersey: Transaction Publishers.

Koob, G. F. (2008). A role for brain stress systems in addiction. *Neuron, 59*, 11-34.

Korte, S. M., Koolhaas, J. M., Wingfield, J. C., & McEwen, B. S. (2005). The Darwinian concept of stress: benefits of allostasis and costs of allostatic load and the trade-offs in health and disease. *Neuroscience and Biobehavioral Reviews, 29*, 3-38.

Kosten, T. A., Zhang, X. Y., & Kehoe, P. (2003). Chronic neonatal isolation stress enhances cocaine-induced increases in ventral striatal dopamine levels in rat pups. *Developmental Brain Research, 141*, 109-116.

Kringelbach, M. L. (2005). The Human Orbitofrontal Cortex: Linking reward to hedonic experience. *Nature Reviews Neuroscience, 6*, 691-702.

Laing, R. D. (1969) *The divided self.* London: Penguin.

Lakoff, G. (2001). How metaphor structures dreams. In Bulkeley, K. (Ed.), *Dreams.* New York: Palgrave.

Lansky, M. R. (1992). The legacy of *The Interpretation of Dreams.* In Lansky, M. R. (Ed.), *Essential papers on dreams.* New York: New York University Press.

Lekners, S., & Tracey, I. (2008). A common neurobiology for pain and pleasure. *Nature Reviews Neuroscience 9*, 314-320.

Lenski, G. E. (1984). *Power and privilege: A theory of social stratification.* Chapel Hill, NC: The University of North Carolina Press.

Levinson, D. F. (2006). The genetics of depression: A review. *Biol Psychiatry, 60*, 84-92.

Liebenberg, L. (2006). Persistence hunting by modern hunter-gatherers. *Current Anthropology, 47* (6), 1017-1025.

Liu, Q-s., Pu, L., & Poo, M-m. (2005). Repeated cocaine exposure *in vivo* facilitates LTP induction in midbrain dopamine neurons. *Nature, 437*, 1027-1031.

Lowen, A. (1985). *Narcissism.* New York: Touchstone.

Luecken, L. J., & Lemery, K. S. (2004). Early caregiving and physiological stress responses. *Clinical Psychology Review, 24*, 171-191.

Luecken, L. J., & Appelhans, B. M. (2006). Early parental loss and salivary cortisol in young adulthood: The moderating role of family environment. *Development and Psychopathology, 18*, 295-308.

Maestripieri, D. (2005). Effects of early experience on female behavioural and reproductive development in rhesus macaques. *Proc. R. Soc. B, 272*, 1243-1248.

Malanga, C. J., Pejchal, M., & Kosofsky, B. E. (2007). Prenatal exposure to cocaine alters the development of conditioned place-preference to cocaine in adult mice. *Pharmacology Biochemistry and Behavior, 87* (4), 462-471.

Marinelli, P. W., Quirion, R., & Gianoulakis, C. (2004). An in vivo profile of B-endorphin release in the arcuate nucleus and nucleus accumbens following exposure to stress or alcohol. *Neuroscience, 127*, 777-784.

Marmot, M. (2004). *The status syndrome.* New York: Henry Holt.

Maynard-Smith, J. (1993). The theory of evolution. London: Penguin.

McNally, R. J. (2006). Cognitive abnormalities in post-traumatic stress disorder. *Trends in Cognitive Sciences, 10* (6), 271-277.

Melville, H. (1851/1964). *Moby-Dick.* Indianapolis, In: Bobbs-Merrill Educational Publishing.

Mitchell, R. L. C., Elliott, R., & Woodruff, P. W. R. (2001). fMRI and cognitive dysfunction in schizophrenia. *Trends in Cognitive Science, 5* (2), 71-81.

Mobbs, D., Greicius, M. D., Abdel-Azim, E., Menon, V., & Reiss, A. L. (2003). Humor modulates the mesolimbic reward centers. *Neuron, 40*, 1041-1048.

Moore-Ede, M. (1993). *The twenty four hour society.* New York: Addison-Wesley.

Morgan, D., Grant, K. A., Gage, H. D., Mach, R. H., Kaplan, J. R., Prioleau, O, et al. (2002). Social dominance in monkeys: dopamine D_2 receptors and cocaine self-administration. *Nature Neuroscience, 5* (2), 169-174.

Nader, M. A., Morgan, D., Gage, H. D., Nader, S. H., Calhoun, T. L., Buchheimer, N., et al. (2006). PET imaging of dopamine D2 receptors during chronic cocaine self-administration in monkeys. *Nature Neuroscience, 9* (8), 1050-1056.

Neborsky, R. J. (2006). Brain, mind and dyadic change processes. *Journal of Clinical Psychology 62* (5), 523-538.

Nelson, E. E., & Panksepp, J. (1998). Brain substrates of infant-mother attachment: Contributions of opioids, oxytocin, and norepinephrine. *Neuroscience and Biobehavioral Reviews, 22* (3), 437-452.

Nesse, R. M., & Young, E. A. (2000). Evolutionary origins and functions of the stress response. *Encyclopedia of Stress, 2*, 79-84.

Nestler, E. J., & Carlezon, W. A. (2005). The mesolimbic dopamine reward circuit in depression. *Biol Psychiatry, 59*, 1151-1159.

Newport, D. J., & Nemeroff, C. B. (2000). Neurobiology of posttraumatic stress disorder. *Current Opinion in Neurobiology, 10*, 211-218.

Nielsen, T. A. & Germain, A. (2000). Post-traumatic nightmares as a dysfunctional state. *Behavioral and Brain Sciences, 23* (6), 978-979.

O'Connor, T. G., & Croft, C. M. (2001). A twin study of attachment in preschool children. *Child Development, 72* (5), 1501-1511.

Oswald, L. M., Zandi, P., Nestadt, G., Potash, J. B., Kalaydjian, A. E., & Wand, G. S. (2006). Relationship between cortisol responses to stress and personality. *Neuropsychopharmacology, 31*, 1583-1591.

Paulus, M. P. (2007). Decision-making dysfunctions in psychiatry – altered homeostatic processing? *Science, 318*, 602-606.

Pesant, N. & Zadra, A. (2006). Dream content and psychological well-being: A longitudinal study of the continuity hypothesis. *Journal Of Clinical Psychology, 62* (1), 111-121.

Piazza, P. V., & Le Maol, M. (1997). Glucocorticoids as a biological substrate of reward: physiological and pathophysiological implications. *Brain Research Reviews, 25*, 359-372.

Pitman, R. K., van der Kolk, B. A., Orr, S. P., & Greenberg, M. S. (1990). Naloxone-reversible analgesic response to combat-related stimuli in posttraumatic stress disorder: A pilot study. *Arch Gen Psychiatry, 47* (6), 541-544.

Pittenger, C., & Duman, R. S. (2008). Stress, depression, and neuroplasticity: A convergence of mechanisms. *Neuropsychopharmacology Reviews, 33*, 88-109.

Plante, D. T., & Winkelman, J. W. (2008). Sleep disturbance in bipolar disorder: Therapeutic implications. *Am J Psychiatry, 165* (7), 830-843.

Pruessner, J. C., Champagne, F., Meaney, M. J., & Dagher, A. (2004). Dopamine release in response to a psychological stress in humans and its relationship to early life maternal care. *The Journal of Neuroscience, 24* (11), 2825-2831.

Raby, C. R., Alexis, D. M., Dickinson, A., & Clayton, N. S. (2007). Planning for the future by western scrub-jays. *Nature, 445*, 919-921.

Read, J. (1998). Child abuse and severity of disturbance among adult psychiatric inpatients. *Child Abuse & Neglect 22*, (5), 359-368.

Reid, S. D. & Simeohn, D. T. (2001). Progression of dreams of crack cocaine abusers as a predictor of treatment outcome: A preliminary report. *The Journal of Nervous and Mental Disease, 189* (12), 854-857.

Ressler, K. J., & Mayberg, H. S. (2007). Targeting abnormal neural circuits in mood and anxiety disorders: From the laboratory to the clinic. *Nature Neuroscience, 10* (9), 1116-1124.

Reuter, J., Raedler, T., Rose, M. Hand, I., Gläscher, J., & Büchel, C. (2005). Pathological gambling is linked to reduced activation of the mesolimbic reward system. *Nature Neuroscience, 8*, 147-148.

Revonsuo, A. (2000). The reinterpretation of dreams: An evolutionary hypothesis of the function of dreaming. *Behavioral and Brain Sciences, 23* (6), 877-901.

Rietschel, M., Beckmann, L., Strohmaier, J., Georgi, A., Karpushova, A., Schirmbeck, F., et al. (2008). G72 and its association with major depression and neuroticism in large population-based groups from Germany. *Am J Psychiatry, 165* (6), 753-762.

Rilling, J. K., Gutman, D. A., Zeh, T. R., Pagnoni, G., Berns, G. S., & Kilts, C. D. (2002). A neural basis for social cooperation. *Neuron, 35*, 395-405.

Robbins, T. W. & Everitt, B. J. (1999). Drug addiction: bad habits add up. *Nature, 398*, 567-570.

Robinson, T. E., & Berridge, K. C. (2003). Addiction. *Annu. Rev. Psychol, 54*, 25-53.

Roitman, M. F., Stuber, G. D., Phillips, P. E. M., Wightman, R. M., & Carelli, R. M. (2004). Dopamine operates as a subsecond modulator of food seeking. *J. Neurosci., 24* (6), 1265-1271.

Saal, D., Dong, Y., Bonci, A., & Malenka, R. C. (2003). Drugs of abuse and stress trigger a common synaptic adaptation in dopamine neurons. *Neuron, 37*, 577-582.

Sandman, C. A., Hetrick, W., Taylor, D. V., & Chicz-DeMet, A. (1997). Dissociation of POMC peptides after self-injury predicts responses to centrally acting opiate blockers. *American Journal on Mental Retardation, 102* (2), 182-199.

Sapolsky, R. M. (2004). *Why zebras don't get ulcers*. New York: Henry Holt.

Sarkar, P., Bergman, K., Fisk, N. M., O'Connor, T. G., & Glover, V. (2007). Ontogeny of foetal exposure to maternal cortisol using midtrimester amniotic fluid as a biomarker. *Clinical Endocrinology, 66*, 636-640.

Schmidt, B. L., Tambeli, C. H., Barletta, J., Luo, L., Green, P., Levine, J. D., & Gear, R. W. (2002). Altered nucleus accumbens circuitry mediates pain-induced antinociception in morphine-tolerant rats. *J. Neurosci., 22* (15), 6773-6780.

Schwartz, M. W., Seeley, R. J. (1997). Neuroendocrine responses to starvation and weight loss. *The New England Journal of Medicine, 336* (25), 1802-1811.

Scott, K. M., Bruffaerts, R., Tsang, A., Ormel, J., Alonso, J, Angermeyer, M. C., et al. (2007). Depression-anxiety relationships with chronic physical conditions: Results from the World Mental Health surveys. *Journal of Affective Disorders, 103*, 113-120.

Sears, W., & Sears, M. (2001). *The attachment parenting book*. New York: Little, Brown and Company.

Segi-Nishida, E., Warner-Schmidt, J. L., & Duman, R. S. (2008). Electroconvulsive seizure and VEGF increase the proliferation of neural stem-like cells in rat hippocampus. *PNAS, 105* (32), 11352-11357.

Selye, H. (1976). *The stress of life*. New York: McGraw-Hill.

Shafton, A. (1995). *Dream Reader: Contemporary approaches to the understanding of dreams*. Albany, NY: State University of New York Press.

Shostak, M. (1981). *Nisa: The life and words of a !Kung woman*. New York: Vintage Books.

Siegel, A., & Bulkeley, K. (1998). *Dreamcatching*. New York: Three Rivers Press.

Singer, T., Seymour, B., O'Doherty, J. P., Stephan, K. E., Dolan, R. J., & Frith, C. D. (2006). Empathic neural responses are modulated by the perceived fairness of others. *Nature, 439*, 466-469.

Siviy, S. M. (1998). Neurobiological substrates of play behavior: Glimpses into the structure and function of mammalian playfulness. In Bekoff, M., & Byers, J. A. (Eds). *Animal play: Evolutionary, comparative, and ecological perspectives*. Cambridge, UK: Cambridge University Press.

Small, D. M., Zatorre, R. J., Dagher, A., Evans, A. C., & Jones-Gotman, M. (2001). Changes in brain activity related to eating chocolate. *Brain, 124*, 1720-1733.

Smith, E. A. (2004). Why do good hunters have higher reproductive success? *Human Nature, 15* (4), 343-364.

Solms, M. (2000). Dreaming and REM sleep are controlled by different brain mechanisms. *Behavioral and Brain Sciences, 23* (6), 843-850.

Sroufe, L. A. (2005). Attachment and development: A prospective, longitudinal study from birth to adulthood. *Attachment & Human Development, 7* (4), 349-367.

Steptoe, A., Feldman, P. J., Kunz, S., Owen, N., Willemsen, G., & Marmot, M. (2002). Stress responsivity and socioeconomic status: A mechanism for increased cardiovascular disease risk? *European Heart Journal, 23*, 1757-1763.

Strong, M. (1998). *A bright red scream: Self-mutilation and the language of pain*. New York: Penguin.

Suddendorf, T., & Corballis, M. C. (1997). Mental time travel and the evolution of the human mind. *Genetic, Social, and General Psychology Monographs, 123* (2), 133-167.

Susskind, J. M., Lee, D. H., Cusi, A., Feiman, R., Grabski, W., & Anderson, A. K. (2008). Expressing fear enhances sensory acquisition. *Nature Neuroscience, 11* (7), 843-850.

Suzuki, D. T. (1960). *Manual of Zen Buddhism*. New York: Grove Press.

Thornberg, F. A., & Lyvers, M. (2006). Attachment, fear of intimacy and differentiation of self among clients in substance disorder treatment facilities. *Addictive Behaviors, 31*, 732-737.

Thornberg, F. A., & Lyvers, M. (2006b). Negative mood regulation (NMR) expectancies, mood, and affect intensity among clients in substance disorder treatment facilities. *Addictive Behaviors, 31*, 811-820.

Tsankova, N., Renthal, W., Kumar, A., & Nestler, E. J. (2007). Epigenetic regulation in psychiatric disorders. *Nature Reviews Neuroscience, 8*, 355-367.

Turnbull, C. M. (1965). *Wayward servants: The two worlds of the African Pygmies.* New York: Natural History Press.

Uhl, G. (2007). Premature poking: Impulsivity, cocaine and dopamine. *Nature Medicine, 13* (4), 413-414.

Ungless, M. A., Singh, V., Crowder, T. L., Yaka, R., Ron, D., & Bonci, A. (2003). Corticotropin-releasing factor requires CRF binding protein to potentiate NMDA receptors via CRF receptor 2 in dopamine neurons. *Neuron, 39*, 401-407.

van der Kolk, B. A., & Greenberg, M. S. (1987). The psychobiology of the trauma response: Hyperarousal, constriction, and addiction to traumatic reexposure. In van der Kolk, B. A., *Psychological Trauma.* Washington, DC: American Psychiatric Press.

van der Kolk, B. A., Greenberg, M. S., Orr, S. P., & Pitman, R. K. (1989). Endogenous opioids, stress induced analgesia, and posttraumatic stress disorder. *Psychopharmacol Bull, 25* (3), 417-421.

van der Kolk, B. A. (2001). The psychobiology and psychopharmacology of PTSD. *Hum Psychopharmacol Clin Exp, 16*, S49-S64.

van der Kolk, B. A. (2003). Posttraumatic stress disorder and the nature of trauma. In M. F. Solomon & D. J. Siegel (Eds.), *Healing Trauma: attachment, mind, body, and brain.* New York: W. W. Norton.

Volkow, N. D. & Fowler, J. S. (2000). Addiction, a Disease of Compulsion and Drive: Involvement of the orbitofrontal cortex. *Cereb Cortex, 10 (3)*, 318-325.

Volkow, N. D., & Li, T-K. (2004). Drug addiction: the neurobiology of behaviour gone awry. *Nature Reviews Neuroscience, 5*, 963-970.

Volkow, N. D., & Wise, R. A. (2005). How can drug addiction help us understand obesity? *Nature Neuroscience, 8* (5), 555-560.

Vyazovskiy, V. V., Cirelli, C., Pfister-Genskow, M., Faraguna, U., & Tononi, G. (2008). Molecular and electrophysiological evidence for net synaptic potentiation in wake and depression in sleep. *Nature Neuroscience, 11* (2), 200-208.

Walsh, T., McClellan, J. M., McCarthy, S. E., Addington, A. M., Pierce, S. B., Cooper, G. M., et al. (2008). Rare structural variants disrupt multiple genes in neurodevelopmental pathways in schizophrenia. *Science, 320*, 539-543.

Wand, G. S., Oswald, L. M., MCCaul, M. E., Wong, D. F., Johnson, E., Zhou, Y, et al. (2007). Association of amphetamine-induced striatal dopamine release and cortisol responses to psychological stress. *Neuropsychopharmacology, 32*, 2310-2320.

Wang, G-J, Volkow, N. D., Logan, J., Pappas, N. R., Wong, C. T., Zhu, W., Netusil, N., & Fowler, J. S. (2001). Brain dopamine and obesity. *The Lancet, 357*, 354-357.

Weaver, I. C. B., Meaney, M. M., & Szyf, M. (2006). Maternal care effects on the hippocampal transcriptome and anxiety-mediated behaviors in the offspring that are reversible in adulthood. *PNAS, 103* (9), 3480-3485.

Williams, L. (1980). *The dancing chimpanzee: A study of the origins of primitive music.* New York: Schoken Books.

Winnicott, D.W. (1986). *Home is where we start from.* New York: Norton.

Wise, R. A. (2002). Brain reward circuitry: Insights from unsensed incentives. *Neuron, 36*, 229-240.

Wong, M-L., Kling, M. A., Munson, P. J., Listwak, S., Licinio, J., Prolo, P., et al. (2000). Pronounced and sustained central hypernoradrenergic function in major depression with melancholic features: Relation to hypercortisolism and corticotropin-releasing hormone. *PNAS, 97* (1), 325-330.

Wright, R. (1994). *The Moral Animal.* New York: Vintage.

Yavich, L., & Tiihonen, J. (2000). Ethanol modulates evoked dopamine release in mouse nucleus accumbens: Dependence on social stress and dose. *European Journal of Pharmacology, 401*, 365-373.

Yeo, R. A., Gangestad, S. W., Edgar, C., & Thoma, R. (1999). The evolutionary genetic underpinnings of schizophrenia: the developmental instability model. *Schizophrenia Research, 39*, 197-206.

Zadra, A., Desjardins, S., & Marcotte, E. (2006). Evolutionary function of dreams: A test of the threat simulation theory in recurrent dreams. *Consciousness and Cognition, 15*, 450-463.

Zhang, T-Y., Parent, C., Weaver, I., & Meaney, M J. (2004). Maternal programming of individual differences in defensive responses in the rat. *Ann. N.Y. Acad. Sci., 1032*, 85-103.

Zink, C. F., Tong, Y., Chen, Q., Bassett, D. S., Stein, J. L., & Meyer-Lindenberg, A. (2008). Know your place: Neural processing of social hierarchy in humans. *Neuron, 58*, 273-283.

Zonnevylle-Bender, M. J. S., Van Goozen, S. H. M., Cohen-Kettenis, P. T., Jansen, L. M. C., Van Elburgt, A., & Van Engeland, H. (2005). Adolescent anorexia nervosa patients have a discrepancy between neurophysiological responses and self-reported emotional arousal to psychosocial stress. *Biological Psychology, 73*, 72-89.

Zubieta, J-K., Smith, Y. R., Bueller, J.A., Kilbourn, M. R., Jewett, D. M., Meyer, C. R., et al. (2001). Regional mu opioid receptor regulation of sensory affective dimensions of pain. *Science, 293*, 311-315.